Embrace the Future

AI's Role in Workplace Excellence

Self Published

Library of Congress Cataloging-in-Publication Data Names: Ambers, Melissa Embrace the Future: AI's Role in Workplace Excellence.

ISBN: 9798876371881

Disclaimer: The content of this book, "Embrace the Future: AI's Role in Workplace Excellence," discusses concepts related to artificial intelligence (AI) and digital and operational transformation. It is important to note that the application and implementation of AI and digital transformation strategies involve various technical, ethical, and operational considerations. The information presented in this book is intended for educational purposes.

It should not be interpreted as professional advice, recommendations, or endorsements for specific AI technologies or digital transformation initiatives. The author and publisher do not assume any responsibility for the outcomes or consequences of using or applying the concepts discussed herein without seeking consultants with expertise.

The information provided in this book may be partial, and specific circumstances may require tailored solutions and strategies depending on your business needs. Furthermore, the field of AI, Digital, & Operational Transformation is continuously evolving, and the information contained in this book may need to be updated over time. Readers should exercise their judgment and discretion when considering the relevance and applicability of the content to their specific situations.

Printed in the United States of America, 2024

Contents

With heartfelt gratitude to Yvette Oldacre, Cheryl Parks, Carolyn Yusufu, Coach Jeff Heggie, Dr. Elizabeth Carter, PhD., CPCU, & Michaelene Holder-March Dr.(H.C) RN, RM, LLB (Hons)MSc IAEM, FCMi, FInstAM, FInstLM – my unwavering circle of support.

Your presence surrounds me, your wisdom guides me, and your honesty calls me out when needed.

Thank you for being the pillars that held up my journey, kept me focus, & being available.

Introduction

Welcome to the dawn of a new era in the world of work. The future has arrived, and its name is Artificial Intelligence, or AI. In the pages that follow, we'll explore how AI is not just a buzzword or a futuristic concept; it's a catalyst for achieving workplace excellence.

The pace of technological change is accelerating at an unprecedented rate, and organizations that harness the power of AI are poised to lead the way. But embracing AI isn't just about adopting the latest technology; it's about embracing a new mindset, understanding the synergy between humans and machines, and dispelling common misconceptions.

Operational transformation is at the heart of this journey. It's the marriage of operational and digital transformation, and AI is the engine driving this transformation forward. This book is your guide to understanding why operational transformation is crucial and how AI can make it a reality.

Fear of the unknown is natural, especially when it comes to new technology. We'll address common fears and misconceptions about AI and illustrate why they shouldn't hold you back. The paradigm shift we advocate isn't about abandoning your past experiences; it's about unlearning old practices to make way for something even better.

But there's more to this AI revolution than just automation. We'll delve into the role of emotional intelligence in the age of AI, showcasing how it can be enhanced through collaboration with machines, creating a harmonious blend of human and artificial intelligence.

In the chapters that follow, we'll provide a roadmap for embracing AI in your workplace. You'll discover strategies for implementing AI, nurturing an AI-ready workforce, and setting the stage for transformation. This book is your key to unlocking the potential of AI, and we're excited to embark on this journey with you.

Get ready to embrace the future. AI is not the future—it's the present, and it's time to make the most of it. Let's embark on this transformative journey together.

Chapter 1
Embracing AI for Operational and Digital Transformation

In this chapter, we will explore the pivotal convergence of operational and digital transformation and how AI is the dynamic catalyst for change. Discover the extraordinary power of AI in driving operational excellence and digital transformation, setting the stage for the transformative journey ahead.

The Convergence of Operational and Digital Transformation

In the ever-evolving landscape of business, two forces have become central to an organization's success: operational transformation and digital transformation. These two concepts were once considered separate endeavors, each with its own goals and strategies. Operational transformation focuses on **streamlining business processes**, **optimizing efficiency**, and **reducing costs**, while digital transformation centers on leveraging technology to **enhance** decision-making, **customer experiences**, and market adaptability.

Today, these two transformational journeys have converged, forming a powerful synergy that propels organizations into the future. Operational transformation alone is no longer sufficient in a digitally-driven world, and digital transformation without operational efficiency lacks the depth needed for lasting change.

The Limitations of Operational Transformation in the Digital Age

In the past, operational transformation was the cornerstone of many organizations' efforts to improve efficiency and reduce costs. It involved streamlining processes, optimizing workflows, and enhancing productivity. While these initiatives yielded significant benefits, they often **operated within the boundaries** of existing technologies and systems.

However, in the digitally-driven world we find ourselves in today, simply fine-tuning operational processes is no longer enough to maintain a competitive edge.

Here's why:

Rapid Technological Advancements: The digital landscape evolves at an astonishing pace. What was considered cutting-edge technology just a few years ago may now be outdated. Operational transformation, while valuable, often focuses on **making the most of existing technology rather than embracing the latest innovations.**

The Need for Data-Driven Decisions: In the digital age, data is king. Organizations that thrive are those that can **harness the power of data to make informed decisions.** This requires not only efficient operations but also a robust digital infrastructure for data collection, analysis, and interpretation.

<u>The Integration of Customer-Centricity</u>: In today's digitally connected world, customer expectations have evolved. Operational transformation alone may not address the need for personalized, **data-driven customer experiences** that set businesses apart.

<u>Market Agility and Adaptability</u>: The ability to **pivot quickly** in response to market changes, trends, and disruptions is essential. Operational transformation might **enhance efficiency**, but digital transformation **empowers organizations** to adapt rapidly to ever-changing conditions.

<u>Competitive Pressures</u>: Industry disruptors often leverage digital technology to challenge traditional business models. To remain competitive, organizations must embrace digital transformation as part of their strategic vision.

In essence, the digital era calls for more than operational streamlining; it calls for a **comprehensive approach** that integrates digital transformation. By doing so, organizations position themselves to thrive in a world where technology and data are at the forefront of success. This convergence of operational and digital transformation forms the basis of a new and exciting journey towards **workplace excellence**, in which AI plays a pivotal role.

The Interdependence of Digital Transformation and Operational Excellence

In today's rapidly changing business landscape, digital transformation has emerged as a critical driver of innovation and competitive advantage. However, it's crucial to understand that digital transformation alone, while pivotal, may fall short of achieving lasting change and comprehensive excellence.

Here's why:

Operational Efficiency as the Backbone: Operational efficiency forms the **backbone of any successful organization**. Without it, even the most advanced digital tools and strategies can't fully flourish. Operational excellence ensures that the foundations of an organization are robust, processes are streamlined, and **resources are optimized**.

Holistic Transformation: True transformation involves a holistic approach that doesn't focus solely on the digital realm. While digital transformation enhances customer experiences, data utilization, and innovation, operational efficiency complements these advancements by ensuring that daily operations are conducted seamlessly and with **minimal waste**.

Long-Term Sustainability: Sustainability in the digital age isn't just about adopting the latest technology. It's about **creating an ecosystem** where efficiency and innovation go hand-in-hand. Operational efficiency contributes to long-term sustainability by reducing costs, improving resource management, and **making the best use of technology investments**.

Adaptability and Agility: In a rapidly evolving digital landscape, organizations need the capacity to **adapt quickly**. Operational excellence **provides the agility required to pivot** and respond to changing market conditions, emerging technologies, and unexpected challenges.

Data-Driven Decision-Making: Digital transformation relies heavily on data-driven decision-making. To make the most of this data, organizations must have **robust operational processes** for data collection, analysis, and utilization. Operational efficiency ensures that data flows smoothly, supporting effective decision-making.

While digital transformation is essential in today's business environment, it **must be closely integrated with operational excellence** to realize its full potential. The two are interdependent, working together to create a resilient, innovative, and sustainable organization. This interdependence forms the core message of this book, emphasizing how organizations can harmonize these two critical aspects to achieve lasting change and workplace excellence.

The Digital Transformation Roadmap Framework

In the ever-evolving landscape of the digital era, organizations are faced with a transformative journey. The road to digital transformation is a complex, yet highly rewarding endeavor. To help you navigate this path with clarity and purpose, we present the "Digital Transformation Roadmap" – a strategic framework designed to guide you through the intricacies of digital transformation.

In this chapter, we will delve into the core of digital transformation, uncovering the essential steps and strategies that can pave the way to sustainable change. The Digital Transformation Roadmap is not just a theoretical construct; it's a practical, actionable guide to catalyze and sustain your journey into the digital age.

This framework is your compass, your tool for strategic planning, and your key to ensuring that digital transformation becomes a powerful agent of change within your organization. Whether you are just beginning your digital transformation journey or seeking to optimize your existing initiatives, this roadmap will provide you with a structured approach, clear objectives, and adaptable strategies.

Throughout this chapter, we will break down the roadmap into phases, each representing a critical juncture in your digital transformation journey. From assessment and planning to cultural transformation, we will explore the specific actions required at each stage. The framework embodies best practices, real-world insights, and the wisdom of successful digital transformation pioneers.

The Digital Transformation Roadmap is your comprehensive guide, your companion in the digital era, and your path to sustainable excellence. It is more than a map; it is your blueprint for change, innovation, and a brighter digital future.

So, let us embark on this transformative journey together, as we dive into the intricacies of the Digital Transformation Roadmap, empowering you to lead your organization into the digital era with confidence and vision.

Phase 1: Assessment and Planning

- Assess Current State: Evaluate the organization's existing processes, systems, and culture.

- Define Objectives: Clearly outline the goals and objectives of the digital transformation.

Phase 2: Strategy Development

- Digital Strategy Formulation: Create a comprehensive strategy that aligns with the organization's goals.

- Leadership Alignment: Ensure leadership is on board and aligned with the digital strategy.

Phase 3: Resource Allocation and Skill Enhancement

- Allocate Resources: Allocate the necessary budget, personnel, and technology resources.

- Upskilling and Reskilling: Identify skills gaps and implement training programs to enhance employee capabilities.

Phase 4: Implementation

- Pilot Initiatives: Start with small-scale pilot projects to test the digital strategy.

- Full Implementation: Roll out digital initiatives across the organization.

Phase 5: Monitoring and Adaptation

- Performance Metrics: Define key performance indicators (KPIs) to measure the success of digital initiatives.

- Continuous Improvement: Continuously assess and adapt strategies and initiatives based on performance data.

Phase 6: Cultural Transformation

- Cultural Shift: Promote a culture of innovation, adaptability, and collaboration.

- Employee Engagement: Engage employees in the transformation process, fostering a sense of ownership.

Summarize the framework's role in achieving sustainable digital transformation and its long-term impact on the organization.

This framework provides a structured approach for organizations to navigate digital transformation, ensuring that it's both impactful and sustainable. It emphasizes continuous improvement, cultural transformation, and employee engagement, which are crucial for long-term success in the digital era. Readers can use this framework as a guide for their digital transformation efforts.

The AI Revolution: Catalyst for Change

As these transformations converged, they found a catalyst that could drive them forward at an unprecedented pace: Artificial Intelligence, or AI. AI is more than just a technology; it's a transformative force **reshaping the way we work**, make decisions, and interact with data. **AI is the engine that takes operational and digital transformation to new heights**, allowing businesses to achieve excellence on previously unattainable levels.

AI is not a passive tool but an active partner in operational and digital transformation. It can analyze vast datasets in real time, make predictions, and optimize operations autonomously. This ability **revolutionizes how organizations operate**, automating routine tasks, providing data-driven insights, and enhancing overall productivity.

The Power of AI in Achieving Workplace Excellence

The true power of AI lies in its potential to **unlock workplace excellence**. AI doesn't merely support existing processes; it revolutionizes them. With the right strategies, it can enhance not just efficiency but effectiveness, driving businesses to new heights of achievement. AI's role in achieving workplace excellence is the central theme of this book.

In the chapters that follow, we'll explore how organizations can not only adapt to this new era but also thrive in it. We'll address the common fears and misconceptions surrounding AI, offer strategies for unlearning and relearning, and emphasize the critical role of emotional intelligence in this AI-augmented world. We'll provide a roadmap for embracing AI, nurturing an AI-ready workforce, and setting the stage for ongoing transformation.

Reshaping Work: Unlocking Workplace Excellence with AI

In the ever-evolving landscape of work, AI stands as the catalyst reshaping not only how we work but also unlocking the path to workplace excellence.

Here's a closer look at how AI is accomplishing this transformation:

<u>Redefining Roles and Responsibilities</u>: AI's automation capabilities are redefining traditional job roles. Mundane and repetitive tasks are entrusted to AI, allowing human workers to **focus on tasks that require creativity, critical thinking, and complex problem-solving**. This reshaping of roles is key to unlocking the full potential of human resources.

<u>Data-Driven Precision</u>: AI thrives on data, processing and analyzing it with unparalleled precision. This data-driven approach reshapes decision-making, enabling organizations to **make informed, accurate choices**. By **reducing guesswork**, businesses can operate with greater efficiency, effectiveness, and confidence.

Customized Experiences: AI personalized products, services, and interactions based on individual preferences and behavior. This reshaping of customer experiences **enhances satisfaction and loyalty**. Tailored solutions lead to more meaningful interactions, ultimately unlocking excellence in customer engagement.

Operational Streamlining: AI's ability to **identify operational inefficiencies reshapes work processes**. By optimizing workflows, reducing errors, and streamlining resource allocation, organizations **unlock operational excellence**. This results in cost savings, resource optimization, and higher efficiency.

Continuous Learning and Growth: AI introduces adaptive learning and development programs. This **reshapes work culture** by fostering a mindset of unlearning and relearning. Employees have the opportunity to continuously acquire new skills and grow, contributing to workplace excellence.

Collaborative Synergy: Work is no longer **limited to human efforts alone**. AI becomes a **collaborative partner, reshaping teams and workflows**. The synergy between human creativity and AI's precision unlocks workplace excellence through innovation and problem-solving.

Embracing the Unfamiliar: The AI-infused workplace encourages a culture of embracing the unfamiliar. It reshapes work by **promoting adaptability and a willingness to learn** and **adapt to change**. This is the cornerstone of excellence in the dynamic digital age.

Augmenting Emotional Intelligence: AI is not just about data and automation; it can also be trained to understand and **respond to human emotions**. This reshapes work by bringing emotional intelligence into the workplace and enhancing employee and customer experiences.

In this era of AI-driven workplace transformation, the reshaping of work as we know it leads to the unlocking of workplace excellence. **AI doesn't replace humans** but complements their abilities, making the workforce more capable, efficient, and innovative. This book is your guide to understanding how this reshaping unfolds, the synergistic relationship between humans and AI, and how it ultimately unlocks the path to workplace excellence. The transformative power of AI is redefining how we work, and by embracing it, we can unlock excellence in our organizations.

Welcome to the AI revolution. It's a journey of convergence, transformation, and ultimately, excellence. This book is your guide to making the most of this transformative era. So, let's embark on this enlightening journey, where we'll embrace the future and unlock the true potential of AI in achieving workplace excellence.

As we stand at the threshold of the digital era, I, as the author, find myself in a unique position—one that allows me to understand the pressing need for a resource like this.

The digital era is characterized by rapid change, constant innovation, and the relentless pursuit of excellence. Melissa and I, as inhabitants of this era, recognize the imperative to provide you, the reader, with a guide to navigating the uncharted waters of AI's transformative potential.

Welcome to the AI revolution. It's a journey of convergence, transformation, and ultimately, excellence. This book is your compass, your key to making the most of this transformative era. Together, let's embark on this enlightening journey, where we'll embrace the future and unlock the true potential of AI in achieving workplace excellence.

I will not leave you on this journey.

Warm Regards,

Digital Era

Chapter 2
Understanding AI's Role in
Workplace Excellence

In our journey to embrace the future of work, we've explored the convergence of operational and digital transformation. Now, we take a deeper dive into the role of Artificial Intelligence (AI) as the linchpin in achieving workplace excellence. AI is not merely a buzzword; it's a transformative force that has reshaped the way we work. In this chapter, we will dissect AI's pivotal role and its symbiotic relationship with operational excellence and digital transformation, uncovering how it drives workplace excellence to new heights.

Operational Transformation: Streamlining Business Processes

Operational transformation is the cornerstone of a well-functioning organization. It's about **streamlining business processes, reducing redundancy, and optimizing workflow**. But in the digital era, this transformation goes beyond traditional process improvement; it's about reshaping operations through AI's intervention.

<u>Automation of Routine Tasks</u>: One of the hallmarks of operational transformation with AI is the automation of routine and repetitive tasks. AI-powered systems excel at handling these mundane processes, **liberating human employees to focus on more strategic and creative endeavors.**

<u>Efficiency Through AI-Driven Insights</u>: AI doesn't just automate; it also provides insights. By analyzing data in real-time, AI can **pinpoint inefficiencies in operations,** propose improvements, and make proactive adjustments, increasing overall efficiency.

<u>Resource Optimization</u>: Effective operational transformation is also about optimal resource allocation. **AI helps organizations make the most efficient use of their resources,** whether it's personnel, time, or equipment.

Digital Transformation: Data-Driven Decision-Making

Digital transformation is synonymous with data. In a digital world, data is the lifeblood of every organization, and it's the **driving force behind decision-making and customer-centricity.**

AI plays an integral role in leveraging data for digital transformation.

<u>Data Collection and Analysis</u>: AI systems are adept at collecting, processing, and analyzing vast amounts of data with unparalleled speed and accuracy. This reshapes how organizations handle data, enabling them to **make data-driven decisions.**

<u>Predictive and Prescriptive Insights</u>: Beyond analysis, AI provides predictive and prescriptive insights. It not only tells you what's happening now but also offers recommendations for the future.

This capability shapes decision-making by **reducing uncertainty**.

Enhanced Customer Experiences: **Customer-centricity is a defining feature of digital transformation.** AI personalized customer experiences based on data-driven insights, creating more meaningful interactions and increasing customer satisfaction.

Streamlining Business Processes: Unleashing Efficiency and Productivity

Streamlining business processes is a fundamental strategy for optimizing operations and achieving excellence in the modern workplace. It's about simplifying, improving, and automating workflows to **enhance efficiency and productivity**.

Here's a more in-depth look at this critical aspect of operational transformation:

Identification of Inefficiencies: The first step in streamlining business processes involves **identifying bottlenecks, redundancies, and areas where efficiency can be improved.** This often requires a comprehensive analysis of existing processes and workflows.

Optimization through Automation: Once inefficiencies are identified, automation becomes a **powerful tool for streamlining**. Tasks that are routine and repetitive can be automated, reducing the margin for human error and speeding up processes.

<u>Resource Allocation</u>: Streamlining processes isn't just about speed; it's also about using resources judiciously. By **optimizing workflows**, organizations can allocate resources more effectively, ensuring that personnel, time, and equipment are used to their fullest potential.

<u>Enhancing Collaboration</u>: Streamlined processes often involve improved collaboration between teams or departments. **Clearer workflows and communication** paths lead to a more cohesive and productive work environment.

<u>Standardization and Best Practices</u>: Part of the streamlining process often includes standardizing procedures and implementing best practices. This reduces variation and ensures consistency in operations, which is **essential for high-quality outcomes**.

<u>Continuous Improvement</u>: Streamlining business processes is not a one-time effort. It's an ongoing commitment to continuous improvement. As technology and circumstances change, processes need to be **adapted and refined to maintain efficiency**.

<u>Data-Driven Insights</u>: The integration of data and analytics plays a **crucial role in process optimization**. Data-driven insights enable organizations to make informed decisions regarding process improvement, as well as measure the impact of these changes.

In the context of AI and workplace excellence, AI's ability to analyze data and automate tasks becomes a powerful ally in streamlining business processes. By letting AI handle routine tasks, employees can **focus on more strategic and creative endeavors**, as discussed earlier. This dynamic partnership between AI and process optimization is a significant driver of workplace excellence, where streamlined processes ensure that the workforce can allocate their skills and resources optimally to achieve the organization's goals.

The Symbiotic Relationship Between AI and Operational Excellence

The synergy between AI, operational transformation, and digital transformation is where true workplace excellence resides. AI optimizes operations, providing efficiency and cost savings. It empowers data-driven decisions in digital transformation, **enhancing customer experiences**.

As we continue our journey, we'll continue to explore real-world examples and actionable strategies for implementing AI in your organization. By understanding this symbiotic relationship, we can **harness the full potential of AI**, operational transformation, and digital transformation to achieve lasting workplace excellence.

In this chapter, we've embarked on a journey of understanding the transformative role of Artificial Intelligence (AI) in **reshaping the way we work** and, ultimately, in unlocking workplace excellence. AI isn't just a tool; it's a catalyst that drives both operational and digital transformation to new heights.

We've explored how AI automates routine tasks, liberating human employees to focus on more strategic and creative endeavors. This **shift from monotonous work to tasks that require creativity and critical thinking is at the heart of workplace excellence**.

Operational transformation, which **streamlines business processes**, and digital transformation, driven by **data-driven decision-making**, are integral components of the AI-driven workplace. These transformations converge in a symbiotic relationship with AI, reshaping the landscape of work.

As we continue our journey, we'll delve deeper into practical applications and real-world examples that showcase how AI can be harnessed for operational excellence and strategic decision-making.

By understanding the pivotal role of AI in workplace excellence, we're poised to navigate the uncharted territories of the digital age and unlock the full potential of human-AI collaboration. The future of work is here, and it's driven by AI, operational excellence, and a commitment to excellence.

"Resisting change is like trying to swim against the tide with an anchor tied to your ankle. Embrace the future; it might just be the life jacket your business needs".

Melissa Ambers, LSS, PMP, PR

Chapter 3
Demystifying AI: Why You Shouldn't Fear the Future

In the grand narrative of technological progress, AI, or Artificial Intelligence, stands as both an alluring promise and an enigmatic force. For some, it's a harbinger of a bright future, while for others, it's shrouded in myths and fears. In this chapter, we embark on a mission to demystify AI, to reveal it not as an adversary but as an ally, a driving force behind the future of work.

We'll start by debunking the myths that have cast shadows of doubt on AI's role in our lives. Then, we'll explore the true nature of AI-human collaboration, highlighting the synergistic approach that defines the modern workplace. Finally, we'll delve into a fundamental truth: AI isn't here to replace humans but to reshape jobs and unlock human potential. The future is not to be feared; it's to be embraced, with AI as our trusted companion.

Debunking AI Myths

AI has long been accompanied by many myths, ranging from job-stealing robots to machines that outsmart their human creators. In this section, we'll debunk these myths, separating fact from fiction, and reveal the **true potential of AI** as a complement to human capabilities.

Separating Fact from Fiction

In the world of AI, myths and misconceptions have proliferated, casting a shadow of doubt over the technology's true potential. It's essential to separate fact from fiction and dispel these myths to **understand AI's role in shaping the future of work accurately**.

Myth 1:

AI Replaces Humans: One of the most prevalent myths about AI is that it's here to replace humans. In reality, AI is designed to complement human abilities, not supplant them. While AI excels at automating routine tasks, it's humans who bring creativity, emotional intelligence, and strategic thinking to the table. The true power of AI emerges when it collaborates with humans, amplifying their capabilities.

Reality:

AI Enhances Humans AI is designed to enhance human capabilities, not replace them. It excels at automating routine tasks, which allows humans to focus on more creative, emotionally intelligent, and strategic aspects of their work. The true power of AI emerges when it collaborates with humans, amplifying their abilities.

Myth 2:

<u>AI Poses a Job Threat</u>: The notion that AI will lead to widespread job losses is another myth that needs debunking. While AI can automate specific tasks, it simultaneously creates new opportunities. AI reshapes job roles by automating the mundane and repetitive, allowing employees to focus on higher-value tasks. Moreover, it fosters the creation of new roles related to AI development, management, and oversight.

Reality:

<u>AI Creates Opportunities</u> AI doesn't necessarily lead to job losses; instead, it creates new opportunities. By automating mundane and repetitive tasks, AI reshapes job roles, enabling employees to concentrate on higher-value activities. Additionally, AI fosters the development of new roles related to its management and oversight.

Myth 3:

<u>AI Is Infallible</u>: Some believe that AI is infallible, always making the right decisions. In truth, AI systems are only as good as the data they are trained on. Bias in data, for example, can lead to biased AI outcomes. Humans are essential in ensuring that AI systems are properly calibrated and used in alignment with ethical guidelines.

Reality:

<u>AI Requires Human Oversight</u> AI systems are not infallible; their performance is contingent on the quality of the data they're trained on. Biases in data can lead to biased AI outcomes. Human judgment and oversight are essential to ensure that AI systems are calibrated correctly and used in alignment with ethical guidelines.

Myth 4:

AI Understands Like Humans: While AI can process vast amounts of data and provide insights, it doesn't possess human-like understanding or consciousness. AI operates based on algorithms and patterns, without true comprehension. This is why human judgment and oversight are crucial to interpreting AI's results correctly.

Reality:

AI Operates on Algorithms AI processes data and provides insights based on algorithms and patterns, but it doesn't possess human-like understanding or consciousness. Human interpretation and judgment are crucial for correctly comprehending AI's results.

Myth 5:

AI Is Only for Tech Experts: Some believe that AI is a domain reserved for technology experts. The reality is that AI is becoming increasingly accessible and user-friendly. Many tools and platforms are designed to be used by professionals in various fields, not just tech specialists.

Reality:

AI Is Accessible to Various Professionals AI is becoming increasingly accessible and user-friendly. Many tools and platforms are designed to be used by professionals in various fields, not just technology specialists. AI is evolving to empower a broader range of professionals to leverage its capabilities effectively.

Debunking these myths lays the foundation for understanding AI's true potential. AI is not a replacement but a transformational force. **It's not a job threat but a job enhancer.** It's not infallible, but it can be harnessed for incredible insights. It's not human-like in understanding, but it augments human capabilities. It's not limited to tech experts but is accessible to professionals across industries. Embracing these truths about AI empowers us to leverage its capabilities effectively and work in harmony with this transformative technology.

AI and Human Collaboration: A Synergistic Approach

AI is not an adversary but a collaborator. In this section, we'll explore how AI and humans can work in harmony, creating a powerful synergy. We'll see that when these two forces come together, the result is not just efficiency, but true workplace excellence.

The collaboration between AI and humans isn't merely a partnership; it's a synergistic relationship that creates a workplace environment where the whole is greater than the sum of its parts. Understanding how AI and humans complement each other is key to unlocking their combined potential.

AI as an Efficiency Enabler: AI's prowess lies in automating routine and repetitive tasks with speed and accuracy. This automation doesn't make humans obsolete; it liberates them from tasks that can be time-consuming and monotonous. This liberation is the first step in creating an environment where human workers can focus on more complex, strategic, and creative activities.

<u>Data-Driven Decision-Making</u>: AI excels in data processing, analysis, and generating insights. By presenting data-driven recommendations, it enhances human decision-making. Human expertise and AI insights create a potent combination. Humans bring contextual understanding, ethical judgment, and creative thinking, while AI ensures that decisions are based on a broad data spectrum.

<u>Innovation and Problem-Solving</u>: The synergy between humans and AI is particularly evident in innovation and problem-solving. AI can process and present vast amounts of information quickly, while humans contribute creativity, critical thinking, and lateral problem-solving abilities. This collaboration leads to innovative solutions and novel approaches that might not be apparent to either AI or humans alone.

<u>Customer-Centric Experiences</u>: In a world where personalization is key, AI can analyze vast customer data to provide tailored experiences. Humans, on the other hand, can infuse these interactions with empathy and nuanced understanding. The result is a customer experience that feels personalized, empathetic, and efficient.

<u>Continuous Learning and Growth</u>: AI plays a crucial role in facilitating continuous learning for employees. It offers adaptive learning experiences and training tailored to individual needs. Human workers can access these resources to improve their skills continually.

<u>Quality Assurance</u>: AI can play a pivotal role in quality assurance by identifying anomalies and potential issues with products or services. Humans oversee and make the final judgment, combining AI's precision with human judgment for the highest quality outcomes.

In essence, AI and human collaboration is a dynamic interplay where AI's capabilities align with human strengths. AI takes on repetitive tasks and data-driven insights, freeing human workers to exercise creativity, emotional intelligence, critical thinking, and strategic decision-making. Together, they create a workplace ecosystem that thrives on the best of both worlds—efficiency and innovation, data and empathy, automation and creativity. This synergistic approach is at the heart of workplace excellence in the digital era, where AI and humans work hand in hand to achieve extraordinary results.

Reshaping Jobs, Not Replacing Humans

Perhaps the most **critical revelation about AI is that it doesn't seek to replace humans**; it seeks to **reshape jobs and empower human potential.** Let's show how AI augments human abilities, automates mundane tasks, and liberates the workforce to focus on creativity, strategic thinking, and growth.

The Augmentation of Human Potential

AI's role in the workforce isn't about replacing humans; it's about reshaping jobs to unlock and augment human potential. This shift in perspective is crucial to understanding the true impact of AI in the workplace.

Automating the Mundane: AI excels at automating routine and repetitive tasks. Mundane tasks often account for a significant portion of an employee's workload. By automating these tasks, AI liberates human workers from the drudgery of repetitive work. This liberation allows employees to focus on tasks that require creativity, strategic thinking, and problem-solving.

The Creative Edge: The essence of human capability lies in creativity, emotional intelligence, and critical thinking. AI can handle logical processes efficiently, but it lacks the spark of creative innovation that humans bring to the table. When AI takes over the mundane, humans are free to channel their creative energies into projects that truly matter.

Strategic Decision-Making: AI's data analysis and insights are invaluable for decision-making, but human judgment and contextual understanding are equally essential. In collaboration, AI provides data-driven recommendations, while humans consider the broader implications, ethical dimensions, and strategic goals of the organization.

Innovation through Collaboration: When AI and humans collaborate, innovation becomes a natural byproduct. AI can process and analyze vast datasets to identify patterns, while humans can see the broader implications and creatively explore new solutions. This collaboration leads to innovative problem-solving and novel approaches that wouldn't be possible with either AI or humans in isolation.

Enhanced Customer Experiences: AI can analyze customer data to personalize experiences, but it's the human touch that adds empathy and a nuanced understanding of individual preferences and emotions. The combination of AI insights and human empathy results in customer-centric interactions that foster satisfaction and loyalty.

Learning and Growth: AI contributes to employee development by offering adaptive learning experiences tailored to individual needs. This approach supports continuous learning and personal growth, ensuring that employees remain adaptable and competent in a changing digital landscape.

Quality Control: AI can excel in quality control by identifying anomalies and potential issues. Human workers then oversee the final judgment, ensuring that the highest quality standards are met. The combination of AI's precision and human judgment results in top-notch quality assurance.

By recognizing the role of AI in reshaping jobs, organizations can **create a workplace environment that capitalizes on the unique strengths of both AI and human employees**. AI takes on the routine and data-driven aspects, freeing human workers to **focus on creativity, empathy, and strategic thinking**. The augmentation of human potential through AI is a fundamental principle in achieving workplace excellence, where humans and machines work in concert to create a more innovative, efficient, and adaptive workforce.

The message is clear.

AI is not the enemy of the future; it's the catalyst for a brighter and more innovative tomorrow. By demystifying the myths, understanding the potential of human-AI collaboration, and embracing the reshaping of jobs, we are better equipped to face the future with confidence.

AI is not to be feared; it's to be harnessed. We will show you throughout this book how it uncovers the true potential of unlocking workplace excellence, proving that the future is not a foe but a friend and that the path to excellence lies in the harmonious collaboration of humans and machines.

AI Is a Tool, Not a Threat: it can be harnessed for positive outcomes. It's a means to improve efficiency, enhance decision-making, and achieve goals.

AI Creates Opportunities: Highlight that AI creates new opportunities. It can open up new career paths, roles related to AI development and management, and innovative solutions that can benefit both individuals and organizations.

AI Enhances Problem-Solving. It can assist in solving complex problems, analyze vast amounts of data, and offer insights that might be beyond human capacity.

AI is a Resource that organizations can leverage to make informed decisions, streamline processes, and deliver better products or services to their customers.

Chapter 4
Pivoting Your Mindset: Unlearning and Relearning

In the ever-evolving landscape of work, the ability to adapt is more crucial than ever. The Age of AI brings with it both opportunities and challenges, demanding a transformation of mindset. In this chapter, we explore the necessity of adaptability and the vital role of unlearning and relearning in thriving in this digital era.

We begin by dissecting the Necessity of Adaptability in the Age of AI, emphasizing how those who can pivot their mindset are better positioned for success. Then, we delve into Cultivating a Culture of Continuous Learning, highlighting the significance of an environment that fosters adaptability and lifelong learning. Finally, we explore the practical side of adapting through the Role of Reskilling and Upskilling, where we equip ourselves with the skills needed to thrive in this new era.

The Necessity of Adaptability in the Age of AI

In a world marked by AI and digital transformation, **adaptability is no longer a desirable trait but a necessity**. The rapid pace of change requires individuals and organizations to be agile and open to new ways of thinking and working.

In the age of AI, adaptability is not just a virtue; it's a vital survival skill. The rapid pace of technological advancements and digital transformation necessitates a fundamental shift in mindset.

Here's a closer look at why adaptability is paramount in this new era:

The Acceleration of Change: The digital era is marked by an unprecedented acceleration of change. New technologies, tools, and platforms emerge at an astounding pace. Businesses that can't **adapt quickly risk falling behind**.

Automation and Job Transformation: AI automates routine tasks, leading to the transformation of job roles. **Adaptability is essential** for individuals to shift from their current roles to new, often more creative or strategic positions.

Embracing Technological Advancements: Individuals and organizations must **embrace new technologies and innovations**. Being open to and proficient with technology is no longer optional; it's a requirement for staying relevant.

Globalization and Connectivity: The interconnected world of business knows no boundaries. Adapting to this global landscape, **understanding diverse cultures, and collaborating with people from around the world are skills that have become essential**.

Lifelong Learning: With the half-life of skills shrinking, the **ability to unlearn and relearn continuously is paramount**. Adaptability means committing to lifelong learning and seeking new knowledge and skills as needed.

Problem-Solving and Critical Thinking: **Adaptability fosters problem-solving and critical thinking**. When individuals are open to change and capable of navigating uncertainty, they're better equipped to address complex challenges.

Agility and Resilience: The ability to pivot in response to unexpected situations and **recover from setbacks** is a hallmark of adaptability. It's about not just surviving but thriving amidst change and adversity.

Innovation and Creativity: Adaptive individuals are more likely to innovate and think creatively. They're **not bound by tradition or a fixed mindset**, but they explore new avenues and possibilities.

Competitive Advantage: In the business world, adaptability is a **competitive advantage**. Organizations that can adapt quickly to market shifts and customer demands are more likely to succeed.

Personal and Professional Growth: On a personal level, **adaptability leads to continuous growth and development**. It fosters a mindset of curiosity and a willingness to take on new challenges.

In the Age of AI, adaptability is the cornerstone of success. It's about embracing change, fostering a growth mindset, and remaining open to new possibilities. Those who can pivot their mindset and thrive amidst change will not just survive but **lead the way in this dynamic digital era**.

Cultivating a Culture of Continuous Learning

The transformation of mindset starts with the creation of a culture that values continuous learning. Understand the importance of fostering an environment that encourages adaptability and lifelong learning. Explore how you can support employees' growth and development.

In the Age of AI, organizations must recognize that adaptability and continuous learning are not just individual traits but collective strengths that lead to workplace excellence.

Cultivating a culture of continuous learning is crucial for organizations that aim to thrive amidst change:

Learning as a Core Value: To foster a culture of continuous learning, organizations must **establish learning as a core value**. It's not just a checkbox on employee training programs; it's a fundamental belief that guides decision-making and behavior.

Leadership Role Modeling: Leaders play a pivotal role in setting the tone for the entire organization. When leaders actively engage in continuous learning, whether by pursuing further education, attending workshops, or seeking feedback, they **inspire others to do the same**.

Investment in Training and Development: Organizations should allocate resources to training and development programs that **empower employees to acquire new skills and knowledge**. This investment reaps dividends in the form of a more adaptable and skilled workforce.

Encouraging Curiosity: A culture of continuous learning encourages curiosity. Organizations should create spaces where **employees feel free to ask questions, explore new ideas, and experiment without fear of failure**.

<u>Feedback and Reflection</u>: Regular feedback and opportunities for reflection are essential for learning and improvement. Encouraging employees to review their work and **seek constructive feedback** contributes to their growth.

<u>Knowledge Sharing</u>: Building a culture where knowledge sharing is encouraged promotes collective learning. When employees share their expertise and experiences, it **enriches the entire organization's knowledge base**.

<u>Adaptable Training Methods</u>: Learning doesn't fit a one-size-fits-all model. **Organizations should adapt training methods** to suit diverse learning styles, whether through traditional classes, online courses, or on-the-job training.

<u>Recognizing and Rewarding Learning</u>: Acknowledging and rewarding employees for their commitment to learning **creates positive reinforcement**. Whether through promotions, special assignments, or recognition programs, it motivates employees to continue learning.

<u>Reskilling and Upskilling Programs</u>: Offering reskilling and upskilling programs allows employees to acquire new skills or enhance existing ones to **meet the organization's evolving needs.** These programs are pivotal in adapting to new technologies and job roles.

<u>Learning from Failure</u>: **Encouraging a culture where failures are seen as learning opportunities rather than setbacks is critical**. It fosters resilience and a willingness to explore innovative solutions.

<u>Monitoring Industry Trends</u>: Staying informed about industry trends and technological advancements is **essential for**

continuous learning. This knowledge helps organizations anticipate changes and adapt proactively.

<u>Support for Lifelong Learning</u>: Organizations should **support employees' pursuit of lifelong learning**, whether it's completing higher education, attending workshops, or engaging in self-paced online courses.

Cultivating a culture of continuous learning is a **long-term commitment that leads to a more adaptable, innovative, and competitive organization**. It's a culture where employees are empowered to embrace change and are equipped with the skills needed to excel in the Age of AI.

The Role of Reskilling and Upskilling

Finally, we get a practical, **understanding of how reskilling and upskilling are pivotal in the Age of AI**. By acquiring new skills and honing existing ones, **individuals can navigate the changing job landscape with confidence and competence**.

As AI transforms the employment landscape and job roles, reskilling and upskilling emerge as crucial strategies for individuals and organizations to navigate change effectively:

<u>Reskilling Defined</u>: Reskilling refers to the process of acquiring new skills or competencies that are entirely different from one's current job role. It often involves a fundamental shift in career focus, allowing individuals to transition to entirely new roles or industries.

<u>Upskilling Defined</u>: Upskilling involves enhancing or expanding existing skills and knowledge within one's current job or industry.

It's about keeping up with changing job requirements and staying competitive in the current role.

Adapting to Job Transformation: In the Age of AI, job roles are continually evolving. Automation and AI technologies may render some tasks obsolete while creating new opportunities. Reskilling allows individuals to adapt to these transformations by acquiring new skills that align with emerging job roles.

Embracing New Technologies: AI and automation often introduce new tools and systems. Upskilling ensures that employees can effectively use these technologies, maximizing their impact and productivity.

Enhancing Employability: Individuals who reskill or upskill are more attractive to employers because they demonstrate a commitment to adapting and evolving in response to industry changes.

Staying Competitive: In a rapidly changing job market, staying competitive requires a commitment to continuous learning and skill development. Upskilling ensures that employees remain relevant in their current roles.

Supporting Organizational Agility: Organizations that invest in reskilling and upskilling programs can quickly adapt to market changes, shifting employee roles to align with evolving needs.

Building a Reskilling Culture: Organizations should establish a culture that supports reskilling and upskilling. This includes offering training programs, encouraging employees to pursue certifications or further education, and providing resources for skill development.

<u>Aligning Skills with Future Needs</u>: Reskilling should align with an individual's and an organization's future goals and needs. Identifying emerging job roles and skills gaps is essential to this alignment.

<u>Investing in Training and Development</u>: Organizations should allocate resources to reskilling and upskilling programs, recognizing that the investment pays off in the form of a more adaptable and competitive workforce.

<u>Support for Lifelong Learning</u>: Encouraging employees to embrace lifelong learning by pursuing new skills, whether it's through traditional education, online courses, or self-directed learning.

<u>Balancing Technical and Soft Skills</u>: Reskilling and upskilling should encompass not only technical skills but also soft skills like communication, leadership, and problem-solving, which are highly valued in the digital era.

The role of reskilling and upskilling is pivotal in ensuring that individuals and organizations can pivot their skill sets in response to the changing employment landscape. It's about staying agile, competitive, and prepared to thrive in the ever-evolving Age of AI.

The AdaptAI Framework: Navigating the Age of AI Through Reskilling and Upskilling

In a world transformed by AI, the AdaptAI framework serves as a comprehensive strategy for individuals and organizations to embrace change, stay competitive, and thrive in the digital era.

Assess Current Skills and Future Needs

Self-Assessment: Start by evaluating your current skills and knowledge. Identify areas where you excel and where you may have skill gaps.

Market Analysis: Stay informed about industry trends, technological advancements, and emerging job roles. Identify the skills that are in demand.

Define Clear Goals

Personal Goals: Define your career aspirations and personal goals. Consider the skills you need to achieve them.

Organizational Goals: Align your goals with those of your organization. What skills does the organization need to stay competitive in the AI-driven landscape?

Acquire New Skills

Reskilling: If your current job role is at risk of automation or becoming obsolete, embark on a reskilling journey. Acquire entirely new skills that align with emerging roles.

Upskilling: Enhance your existing skills to stay competitive in your current role. This involves improving your proficiency in areas where you already have expertise.

Plan and Prioritize Learning

Learning Path: Create a structured learning plan. Choose the courses, resources, and methods that will help you acquire the required skills.

Time Management: Prioritize learning in your schedule. Dedicate specific times for skill development, whether through online courses, workshops, or self-study.

Technology Proficiency

AI Familiarity: Develop a fundamental understanding of AI and its applications within your industry. This knowledge will help you adapt to AI-driven processes.

Technical Skills: Acquire technical skills relevant to your field, whether it's data analysis, programming, or proficiency with industry-specific software.

Apply Learning in Real Contexts

Project Work: Apply your new skills in practical projects. This hands-on experience is invaluable for reinforcing your knowledge.

On-the-Job Application: Seek opportunities to use your skills in your current job role. Discuss potential projects or tasks with your superiors that allow you to apply what you've learned.

Invest in Continuous Learning

Lifelong Commitment: Embrace the idea of continuous learning throughout your career. The digital era demands a lifelong commitment to acquiring new skills.

Professional Development: Attend workshops, conferences, and seminars related to your field. Networking with professionals in your industry can also provide valuable insights.

This AdaptAI framework is **not a one-time strategy but a continuous cycle of learning, adaptation, and growth**. By following this framework, individuals and organizations can effectively navigate the Age of AI, ensuring that they remain adaptable, competitive, and poised for success in the dynamic digital landscape.

Recognizing that **adaptability is not just a desirable skill; it's a cornerstone of success** in the Age of AI. Pivoting one's mindset to embrace continuous learning, unlearning, and relearning is the path to workplace excellence. In the chapters to follow, we'll explore practical strategies for individuals and organizations to adapt, thrive, and remain at the forefront of the digital era. The future is dynamic, and those who pivot their mindset to embrace change will be the ones shaping it.

"Emotional intelligence is the language of leadership. It's the unspoken fluency that sets great leaders apart, enabling them to connect, inspire, and drive excellence in their teams."

Melissa Ambers, LSS, PMP, PR

Chapter 5
The Emotional
Intelligence of AI and
Humans

In an era where technology and artificial intelligence reign, it's easy to focus solely on the quantitative aspects of work. However, the **human factor remains an essential element in workplace** excellence. In this chapter, we explore the Emotional Intelligence (EQ) of both AI and humans, highlighting the crucial role it plays in creating a harmonious and high-performing workplace.

We begin by understanding the EQ Factor in Workplace Excellence, emphasizing how emotional intelligence contributes to **effective collaboration and leadership**. Then, we delve into the concept of human-AI collaboration and the Empathy Connection, exploring how emotional intelligence bridges the gap between humans and machines. Finally, we discuss strategies for Fostering Emotional Intelligence in the AI-enhanced workplace, ensuring that EQ remains a cornerstone of success in the digital age.

The EQ Factor in Workplace Excellence

Emotional intelligence, often abbreviated as EQ, is a defining trait that influences how individuals and teams interact, communicate, and lead. In this section, we explore how EQ contributes to workplace excellence by fostering positive relationships, effective communication, and strong leadership.

Nurturing Emotional Intelligence for Success

Emotional intelligence (EQ) is an indispensable asset in the workplace, often overshadowed by technical skills and qualifications. However, it plays a pivotal role in determining workplace excellence by **fostering positive relationships, enhancing communication, and facilitating strong leadership**:

Building Strong Relationships: In any workplace, success relies on relationships. High-EQ individuals excel in building and maintaining positive relationships. They are **empathetic, good listeners**, and understanding, all of which contribute to a harmonious work environment.

Effective Communication: EQ **enhances communication** by promoting self-awareness and empathy. Individuals with high EQ can express themselves clearly and understand others' perspectives, **reducing misunderstandings and conflicts**.

Conflict Resolution: Workplace conflicts are inevitable, but individuals with high EQ can navigate them with finesse. They understand the emotional dynamics of conflicts, **find common ground, and seek resolutions** that benefit all parties.

Teamwork: High EQ team members are adept at collaboration. They can identify and appreciate the strengths of their colleagues, communicate effectively within the team, and **contribute to a positive team atmosphere.**

Leadership: Leaders with high EQ inspire their teams. They are emotionally attuned to the needs and concerns of their employees, making them approachable and understanding. **This type of leadership fosters employee satisfaction and motivation.**

Stress Management: EQ equips individuals to handle stress effectively. They can identify stress triggers, employ coping mechanisms, and **maintain a level head in high-pressure situations.**

Adaptability: In the ever-changing digital landscape, adaptability is essential. Individuals with high EQ are more **flexible and open to change**, making them more resilient in the face of technological shifts and transformations.

Decision-Making: EQ influences decision-making by enabling individuals to consider not only the facts but also the emotional implications of their choices. This broader perspective often leads to more **balanced and ethical decisions.**

Customer Relations: High EQ individuals excel in customer-facing roles. They can understand and respond to customers' emotions, **leading to better customer experiences** and satisfaction.

Conflict Prevention: EQ isn't only about resolving conflicts but also about preventing them. High-EQ individuals are skilled at identifying potential sources of conflict and addressing them proactively.

Motivation and Productivity: Individuals with high EQ tend to be more motivated and productive. They understand their motivations and those of their colleagues, creating a workplace where **everyone is engaged** and working toward common goals.

Organizational Culture: A strong EQ culture contributes to a positive and inclusive work environment. It sets the tone for how individuals interact, collaborate, and **lead within the organization**.

Nurturing emotional intelligence in the workplace is essential for achieving excellence in the Age of AI. It creates a more harmonious, productive, and adaptive environment where individuals and teams thrive, ultimately leading to the success of the organization.

Human-AI Collaboration: The Empathy Connection

As AI and humans increasingly collaborate, empathy emerges as a **crucial link** between the two. In this section, we examine how emotional intelligence bridges the gap between humans and AI, allowing for smoother interactions, better decision-making, and enhanced teamwork.

The **collaboration between humans and AI is no longer a distant vision of the future; it's a present reality**. In this context, empathy emerges as a critical link that facilitates smoother interactions, better decision-making, and more effective teamwork:

Understanding Emotional Data: AI systems can now analyze emotional data, such as sentiment analysis from customer interactions or facial recognition. This capability **enables AI to understand human emotions and react accordingly**, whether in customer service or personal assistants like chatbots.

Emotional Feedback: By **providing emotional feedback,** AI systems can encourage more empathetic human responses. For instance, a chatbot that recognizes user frustration can adapt its tone to provide more empathetic and understanding responses.

Enhancing User Experience: Empathetic AI enhances user experience in various domains, such as healthcare, where AI can provide emotional support, or in education, where **AI can adapt** its teaching style to match students' emotional states.

Decision Support: In **decision-making processes,** AI can consider emotional factors that might be overlooked by humans. For example, in healthcare, AI can help healthcare providers consider patients' emotional well-being alongside their physical health for more holistic care.

Emotional Resonance: AI's ability to understand and respond to human emotions **creates a sense of emotional resonance.** This emotional connection can improve the overall user experience and lead to more positive interactions.

Mitigating Bias: Emotion-aware AI can help mitigate biases in decision-making. By considering emotional factors, AI systems can ensure that decisions are not solely based on objective data but also **account for the emotional aspects** of a situation.

Adaptive Interfaces: In user interfaces, **AI can adapt** based on the user's emotional state. For example, in a smart home, AI can adjust lighting, music, or temperature to create a more comfortable and emotionally appealing environment.

Conflict Resolution: In a team or organizational context, **AI can assist** in conflict resolution by understanding and mediating emotional aspects of disputes. This can lead to more effective and empathetic solutions.

Cultural Sensitivity: **AI systems can be designed to understand** and respect cultural differences, which often involve varying emotional expressions and norms. This cultural sensitivity can lead to more inclusive AI interactions.

Enhancing Human Skills: Instead of replacing human roles, empathetic **AI systems enhance human skills**. In healthcare, AI can support nurses and doctors by handling routine tasks, allowing them to focus on empathetic care.

Feedback for Improvement: Emotion-aware **AI can provide valuable feedback** to humans on their interactions and emotional impact. This feedback can help individuals develop their emotional intelligence and empathy.

Data Privacy and Trust: The responsible use of emotional data is a critical consideration. **AI systems must respect data privacy and build trust** with users by transparently managing emotional information.

Emotional intelligence in the context of human-AI collaboration is a bridge that connects the capabilities of AI with the human qualities of empathy, understanding, and emotional connection. It transforms the way we interact with technology, making those interactions more humane and effective, ultimately contributing to a more harmonious coexistence between humans and AI.

Fostering Emotional Intelligence in the AI-Enhanced Workplace

Emotional intelligence isn't just an inherent trait; it can be **nurtured and developed**. In this section, we discuss strategies for fostering EQ in the AI-enhanced workplace. These strategies **empower individuals and organizations** to cultivate emotional intelligence as an integral part of their success in the digital era.

Nurturing the Human Element

In a workplace increasingly enhanced by AI, fostering emotional intelligence becomes vital for ensuring that the human element remains at the **core of organizational success**:

Emotional Intelligence Training: Providing emotional intelligence training for employees is essential. This training helps individuals **understand their own emotions**, recognize emotions in others, and effectively manage both.

Emotionally Aware Leadership: Leaders should lead by example. They need to exhibit and **encourage emotional intelligence** in their interactions, decision-making, and communication with their teams.

Team Building with Empathy: **Encourage team-building** activities that promote empathy and understanding among team members. Activities like group discussions, feedback sessions, and empathy training can build stronger and more cohesive teams.

<u>Effective Communication</u>: **Teach effective communication** techniques that include active listening, non-verbal communication, and empathetic responses. Such skills lead to clearer, more meaningful interactions.

<u>Conflict Resolution Workshops</u>: Conflict is inevitable, but teaching employees how to **resolve conflicts with empathy** can prevent disruptions and improve overall workplace dynamics.

<u>Feedback that Fosters Growth</u>: Implement feedback mechanisms that focus on personal and professional growth. This type of feedback **promotes emotional growth, self-awareness, and empathy**.

<u>Mentorship Programs</u>: Pairing employees with mentors who exhibit high emotional intelligence can **provide valuable guidance** and role models for fostering emotional intelligence.

<u>AI-Assisted Training</u>: Use AI to assist in emotional intelligence training. AI can provide **real-time feedback** on tone, communication style, and empathy in employee interactions.

<u>Designing AI with Emotional Sensitivity</u>: Developers should design AI systems with emotional sensitivity in mind. This involves **understanding the emotional aspects of user interactions** and designing AI responses that reflect empathy.

<u>Psychological Safety</u>: Create an environment where employees feel psychologically safe to express their emotions, concerns, and ideas. Psychological safety fosters emotional intelligence by **encouraging open and honest communication**.

<u>Measuring Emotional Intelligence</u>: Implement measures to assess emotional intelligence in the workplace. These assessments can help **identify areas for improvement and track progress**.

<u>Support for Employee Well-Being</u>: **Promote initiatives** that support employee well-being. Well-balanced employees are more likely to exhibit emotional intelligence in their interactions.

<u>Cultivate a Growth Mindset</u>: Encourage a growth mindset among employees, where they **view challenges as opportunities** to learn and grow emotionally. This mindset helps them adapt to changing workplace dynamics.

<u>Emotional Support Programs</u>: Offer emotional support programs for employees who may be **experiencing personal or professional challenges**. These programs can provide resources for emotional well-being.

<u>Recognition of Emotional Efforts</u>: **Recognize and reward employees** who consistently exhibit emotional intelligence. This recognition can serve as an incentive for others to develop their emotional intelligence.

Fostering emotional intelligence in the AI-enhanced workplace creates a work environment that values empathy, understanding, and effective human interaction. It ensures that AI complements, rather than replaces, the **unique human qualities that contribute to workplace excellence**. By **nurturing emotional intelligence**, organizations can embrace the future while keeping the human element at the forefront of their success.

Nurturing the Human Element: An Integrated Approach

In the age of AI, nurturing the human element involves a holistic strategy that combines training, culture-building, and leadership support to ensure that the workplace remains centered on human values and emotional intelligence:

Training for Emotional Intelligence

Comprehensive Emotional Intelligence Training: Implement structured emotional intelligence training programs that cover self-awareness, self-regulation, empathy, and interpersonal skills. These programs should be accessible to all employees.

Customized Learning Paths: Tailor emotional intelligence training to different roles and levels within the organization. For example, leaders may require advanced training in empathetic leadership, while customer-facing roles may need training in customer empathy.

AI-Assisted Training: Leverage AI tools to personalize emotional intelligence training. AI can analyze an individual's interactions and suggest areas for improvement, enabling employees to continuously enhance their emotional intelligence.

Culture-Building for Empathy and Understanding

Leadership as Role Models: Ensure that leaders exemplify emotional intelligence in their interactions and decision-making. Leaders set the tone for the entire organization.

<u>Cultural Norms:</u> Define cultural norms that prioritize empathy, active listening, and conflict resolution. Encourage employees to embrace these norms in their daily interactions.

<u>Team-Building Initiatives</u>: Organize team-building activities that promote empathy and understanding among team members. Such activities create strong bonds, trust, and effective collaboration.

<u>Recognition and Rewards</u>: Recognize and reward employees who consistently exhibit emotional intelligence. This creates a culture that values and reinforces emotional intelligence.

Leadership Support for Emotional Intelligence

<u>Emotionally Aware Leadership Development</u>: Develop leadership programs that emphasize emotional intelligence. Leaders should understand and manage their own emotions while recognizing and responding to the emotions of their teams.

<u>Conflict Resolution Skills</u>: Provide leaders with advanced training in conflict resolution that emphasizes empathy and understanding. Equipped with these skills, leaders can mediate conflicts more effectively.

<u>Mentorship and Coaching</u>: Encourage leaders to mentor and coach their teams in emotional intelligence. This includes providing guidance on managing emotions, building positive relationships, and making emotionally informed decisions.

<u>Continuous Feedback</u>: Implement a feedback mechanism that enables leaders to receive feedback on their emotional

intelligence and leadership style. This feedback helps them refine their emotional intelligence skills.

This integrated approach aims to nurture the human element in the AI-enhanced workplace, ensuring that the organization places a strong emphasis on emotional intelligence, empathy, and understanding. It combines skill development, cultural values, and leadership support to create an environment where AI and humans coexist harmoniously, with human qualities at the forefront of success.

Skill Development for Nurturing the Human Element

Skill development is a **critical aspect of nurturing the human element**, especially in the context of emotional intelligence and empathy. Here's a deeper look at how organizations can develop these skills:

Emotional Intelligence Training: Implement comprehensive emotional intelligence training programs that cater to employees at all levels within the organization:

Self-Awareness: Help employees recognize and understand their emotions, strengths, and areas for improvement. This self-awareness is the foundation of emotional intelligence.

Self-Regulation: Teach employees how to manage their emotions effectively. This includes techniques for staying calm under pressure, handling stress, and regulating their responses.

Empathy: Train employees to recognize and understand the emotions of others. Empathy involves actively listening to colleagues, clients, and peers to better understand their perspectives.

Interpersonal Skills: Provide training in effective interpersonal skills, which encompass clear and empathetic communication, conflict resolution, and building positive relationships.

Customization: Tailor training programs to specific roles within the organization. For example, leaders may require advanced training in empathetic leadership, while customer-facing roles may need training in customer empathy.

Skill development in emotional intelligence is an ongoing journey. It's not a one-time event but a continuous process that involves training, application, feedback, and recognition. By focusing on skill development, organizations can ensure that emotional intelligence and empathy remain integral to their workplace culture, fostering harmonious coexistence with AI and nurturing the human element.

AI-Assisted Personalized Training

Utilize AI technology to personalize emotional intelligence training. AI can analyze individual interactions and provide feedback on areas that need improvement.

AI can offer real-time guidance during interactions, suggesting ways to **enhance emotional intelligence in communication, customer service, or teamwork.**

Machine learning algorithms can adapt training programs based on an individual's progress and specific areas of need, creating a highly personalized learning experience.

Practical Application

It's essential to provide opportunities for employees to apply what they've learned in real work scenarios:

Encourage employees to **practice emotional intelligence** skills in their daily interactions with colleagues, clients, and stakeholders.

Support the **use of emotional intelligence in decision-making, problem-solving, and conflict resolution.**

Create a feedback culture where employees receive constructive input on their emotional intelligence skills, allowing for ongoing improvement.

Mentorship and Coaching

Pair employees with mentors or coaches who excel in emotional intelligence. These mentors can provide guidance and real-life examples of how to apply emotional intelligence in various situations.

Encourage leaders to mentor their teams in emotional intelligence. Leadership's support and guidance are pivotal in developing emotional intelligence at all levels.

Mentorship programs should **focus on not only theoretical knowledge but also practical implementation** and scenario-based learning.

Measuring Progress:

Implement assessments and metrics to measure and **track emotional intelligence** in the workplace. These assessments can help identify areas for improvement and track progress over time.

Regularly review and discuss these assessments with employees, offering specific feedback and development plans.

Feedback and Recognition

Create a feedback mechanism that **encourages employees to provide feedback** on their colleagues' emotional intelligence. This can **promote self-awareness and accountability.**

Recognize and reward employees who consistently exhibit emotional intelligence. Incentives and recognition programs can motivate others to develop their emotional intelligence.

Beyond Dollars: Non-Monetary Rewards that Inspire and Motivate

In the world of employee motivation and retention, it's a common belief that monetary rewards, such as raises and bonuses, are the primary drivers of job satisfaction. While financial incentives certainly play a significant role, the scope of rewarding and motivating employees extends far beyond dollars and cents. In this section, we explore the wide array of non-monetary rewards that can be equally, if not more, effective in inspiring and motivating your workforce.

These non-monetary rewards are built on recognition, personal development, work-life balance, and a supportive work environment. They affirm that **employees are not just contributors to an organization but valued members of a dynamic community**. You'll discover the power of appreciation, personal growth, and a workplace culture that fosters not only professional success but also a sense of belonging and fulfillment. Let's explore how non-monetary rewards can elevate your workforce and drive excellence in your organization.

Here are some options to consider for rewarding employees:

Public Recognition: Acknowledge employees' achievements in team meetings, company-wide emails, or on a bulletin board. Highlight their contributions and celebrate their successes.

Praise and Gratitude: Offer sincere words of appreciation. A simple "thank you" or a personalized note expressing gratitude for their efforts can go a long way in boosting morale.

Flexible Work Arrangements: Provide flexibility in work schedules, such as allowing remote work or offering flexible hours. This can greatly enhance work-life balance and is highly valued by many employees.

Professional Development: Invest in employees' growth by offering opportunities for training, workshops, and courses. Supporting their learning and career development shows a commitment to their long-term success.

Additional Time Off: Reward exceptional performance with additional paid time off, such as an extra day of vacation or a "well-being day" to recharge.

<u>Employee of the Month/Quarter Awards</u>: Recognize outstanding employees with awards or certificates, and feature their achievements prominently within the workplace.

<u>Project Ownership</u>: Assign employees ownership of meaningful projects or initiatives that align with their skills and interests. This gives them a sense of purpose and responsibility.

<u>Task Delegation</u>: Delegate tasks to employees that empower them to take on more significant responsibilities. This shows trust and encourages professional growth.

<u>Mentorship and Career Guidance</u>: Provide employees with mentorship or career guidance sessions. Pair them with experienced colleagues who can offer advice and support in their professional journey.

<u>Team Building and Social Activities</u>: Organize team-building events, social gatherings, or fun activities to foster camaraderie and a positive work atmosphere.

<u>Wellness Programs:</u> Offer wellness benefits, such as gym memberships, yoga classes, or mental health resources. Supporting employees' physical and mental well-being is a valuable form of reward.

<u>Workplace Flexibility</u>: Allow employees to tailor their workspace to their preferences. Providing ergonomic furniture, personalized office decor, or comfortable chairs can enhance job satisfaction.

<u>Challenging Assignments</u>: Assign employees to challenging projects that align with their skills and interests, providing them with opportunities to grow and showcase their talents.

<u>Leadership Opportunities</u>: Recognize leadership potential in employees and offer them opportunities to lead teams, projects, or initiatives.

<u>Work-Life Integration</u>: Encourage work-life integration by respecting boundaries and allowing employees to balance their personal and professional lives.

<u>Casual Dress Days</u>: Implement casual dress days or themed dress-up days to create a more relaxed and enjoyable work environment.

<u>Community Involvement</u>: Support employees' involvement in community service or volunteer activities. This can foster a sense of social responsibility and fulfillment.

<u>Innovation and Idea Recognition</u>: Recognize employees who contribute innovative ideas or suggestions to improve processes or products.

<u>Peer Recognition</u>: Encourage peers to recognize and commend each other for their contributions. Peer-to-peer recognition can be highly meaningful.

<u>Time for Passion Projects</u>: Allow employees to dedicate a portion of their work time to pursue personal passion projects or innovations that align with the organization's goals.

Non-monetary rewards are often about creating a positive, supportive, and appreciative work environment. They show employees that their contributions are valued and that their well-being is a priority. Ultimately, non-financial rewards can be as impactful as monetary incentives in motivating and retaining employees.

As we conclude this chapter on nurturing the human element in the AI-enhanced workplace, we've journeyed through the multifaceted landscape of emotional intelligence, empathy, and the non-monetary rewards that inspire and motivate employees. In the ever-evolving world of work, it's become increasingly clear that success is not solely measured by profits or productivity; it's also about the well-being and growth of the individuals who make it all happen.

We've explored the importance of skill development in emotional intelligence, understanding that by investing in training, mentorship, and a culture of recognition, organizations can elevate their employees' interpersonal and intrapersonal skills. By fostering emotional intelligence, we create not just more effective professionals, but better colleagues, leaders, and individuals.

Furthermore, we've touched on the significance of non-monetary rewards, from public recognition and praise to flexible work arrangements and wellness programs. These initiatives show that in the modern workplace, it's not only about the work itself but also about the people who do the work. Employees are not just assets; they're integral contributors to the organization's success and culture.

In a world where artificial intelligence is increasingly prevalent, the role of human qualities like empathy, understanding, and personal growth becomes all the more critical. Nurturing the human element ensures that employees don't just coexist with AI but thrive alongside it. The result is a workplace that values not just output but the well-being and fulfillment of its workforce. It's a workplace where people are inspired, motivated, and driven to achieve not only professional success but personal growth as well.

As we move forward, remember that these principles of nurturing the human element can have a profound impact on organizational excellence, contributing to the success of your workforce, your organization, and the individuals who make it all possible. In the chapters ahead, we'll continue to explore how these principles apply to the ever-evolving landscape of work and AI.

Steps to Nurturing the Human Element in the AI-Enhanced Workplace

- Leadership Commitment:

  - Ensure leadership is committed to fostering the human element in the workplace.

  - Encourage leaders to exemplify emotional intelligence and empathy in their interactions.

- Emotional Intelligence Training:

  - Provide emotional intelligence training to employees at all levels.

  - Teach self-awareness, empathy, active listening, and conflict resolution.

- Empathy-Centric Culture:

  - Establish an organizational culture that values empathy, understanding, and open communication.

  - Encourage employees to empathize with colleagues, clients, and other stakeholders.

- Effective Communication:

  - Promote effective communication skills that include active listening, non-verbal communication, and empathetic responses.

- Train employees in techniques to enhance the clarity and impact of their communication.

- Mentorship Programs:

  - Implement mentorship programs where employees can learn from mentors who excel in emotional intelligence.

  - Pair employees with mentors who can guide the development of emotional intelligence.

- AI-Assisted Training:

  - Use AI to provide real-time feedback on emotional intelligence during employee interactions.

  - Utilize AI to offer personalized training and improvement suggestions.

- Emotionally Aware Leadership:

  - Develop leadership programs that emphasize emotional intelligence.

  - Encourage leaders to recognize and manage their own emotions and understand those of their teams.

- Conflict Resolution Workshops:

  - Conduct workshops on conflict resolution with an emphasis on empathy and understanding.

- Teach employees how to resolve conflicts in a way that maintains positive relationships.

- **Feedback for Emotional Growth:**

  - Implement feedback mechanisms that focus on personal and emotional growth.

  - Encourage employees to provide constructive feedback that fosters emotional intelligence.

- **Psychological Safety:**

  - Create an environment where employees feel psychologically safe to express their emotions, concerns, and ideas.

  - Encourage open and honest communication by removing fear of judgment or backlash.

- **Measuring Emotional Intelligence:**

  - Use assessments and metrics to measure and track emotional intelligence in the workplace.

  - Identify areas for improvement and monitor progress over time.

- **Cultivate a Growth Mindset:**

- o Promote a growth mindset among employees, encouraging them to view challenges as opportunities for emotional growth.

- o Recognize that developing emotional intelligence is an ongoing journey.

- Support for Employee Well-Being:

  - o Offer well-being initiatives that address employees' physical and mental health.

  - o A balanced, well-supported workforce is better equipped to develop emotional intelligence.

- Emotional Support Programs:

  - o Provide programs that offer emotional support to employees facing personal or professional challenges.

  - o These resources can help employees maintain their emotional well-being.

- Recognition of Emotional Efforts:

  - o Recognize and reward employees who consistently exhibit emotional intelligence.

  - o Use incentives and recognition programs to motivate others to develop their emotional intelligence.

Nurturing the human element in the AI-enhanced workplace requires a multifaceted approach that involves training, culture-building, leadership support, and ongoing measurement. By following these steps, organizations can create an environment where employees and AI systems coexist harmoniously, embracing the unique human qualities that contribute to workplace excellence.

Chapter 6
AI Implementation
Strategies
for Excellence

In the ever-evolving landscape of the modern workplace, the integration of artificial intelligence (AI) is not just a possibility; it's a strategic imperative. AI has the potential to revolutionize operations, enhance decision-making, and drive innovation, making it a vital component of achieving organizational excellence.

In this chapter, we will delve into AI implementation strategies designed to empower your organization to harness the full potential of this transformative technology. We'll explore how to build an AI-ready workforce, set the right priorities for AI integration, and ensure that your AI initiatives align with your overarching strategic goals.

As AI takes its place alongside human talent, the harmonious collaboration between the two becomes a powerful force. It's **not a matter of man versus machine**; it's about **leveraging the unique strengths** of both to achieve workplace excellence. Let's embark on this journey to understand how to effectively implement AI in your organization and drive it toward new heights of success.

AI Adoption: A Strategic Imperative

In a rapidly changing business landscape, organizations that resist AI adoption risk falling behind.

Failing to embrace AI can lead to operational inefficiencies, outdated decision-making processes, and missed growth opportunities.

The fear of job displacement is a common concern, but in reality, AI can complement human work, not replace it.

In the relentless race of modern business, operational efficiency is the engine that propels organizations forward. Without it, businesses can find themselves **stuck in the past**, unable to keep up with the ever-accelerating pace of change. One of the most promising tools for enhancing operational efficiency is artificial intelligence (AI). Yet, many organizations grapple with the decision to embrace AI, often due to the **looming fear of job displacement.**

This chapter is a journey through the challenges and solutions related to AI adoption. Failing to embrace AI can indeed lead to operational inefficiencies, but it's essential to emphasize that this fear of job displacement is often misplaced. The truth is that AI is not here to replace humans; it's here to work alongside us, enhancing our capabilities and driving operational excellence.

By the end of this chapter, you'll not only understand the critical importance of AI adoption but also the **value of creating an AI-human synergy** where both elements work harmoniously to drive operational efficiency and excellence. Let's embark on this enlightening journey.

Without AI, organizations may struggle to stay competitive, leading to potential declines in market share and revenue.

The cost of not adapting to AI may far exceed the cost of adoption. Businesses risk stagnation and becoming irrelevant in their industries.

To address these challenges, AI adoption becomes a strategic imperative. Embracing AI is not just about implementing new technology; it's about **transforming your organization's approach** to work. This transformation necessitates a commitment to building an AI-ready workforce, setting the right priorities for AI integration, and redefining the way you operate.

Building an AI-Ready Workforce

A workforce that lacks AI skills is **ill-prepared for the future.** Employees who feel threatened by AI may resist its implementation, hindering progress.

Without the necessary skills, employees can't fully harness the potential of AI technology.

This resistance can create internal strife and **slow down the adoption process.**

Building an AI-ready workforce involves offering training and development programs that empower employees with AI skills. Employees should be **assured that AI is not a threat** to their roles but a tool that enhances their capabilities. Effective training includes unlearning and relearning, where employees adapt to **new ways of working and leverage AI to improve their performance and eliminate wasted time.**

Preparing Your Team for Success

In the journey towards AI adoption, building an AI-ready workforce is paramount. It's not just about integrating advanced technology into your operations; it's about empowering your team to effectively harness the power of AI. Here are the key elements of this process:

Skills Development:

A lack of AI skills leaves employees ill-prepared for the AI-driven future. Without AI skills, employees can't fully utilize AI technology and are less productive. Offer comprehensive AI training programs that empower employees with AI-related skills. This includes understanding AI principles, data analysis, machine learning, and AI applications in specific job roles.

Cultural Transformation:

A workforce fearing AI may resist its implementation, hindering progress. A culture of **resistance can slow down AI adoption** and create internal strife. Create a culture of AI acceptance and enthusiasm. Assure employees that AI is not a threat to their roles but a tool that enhances their capabilities. Encourage a growth mindset, where employees embrace AI as a means to grow professionally.

Embracing Unlearning and Relearning:

Employees may be hesitant to unlearn old habits and relearn new AI-driven processes. The reluctance to adapt to AI technologies can **hinder the integration process**. Establish a culture of continuous learning. Encourage employees to unlearn old processes and relearn new, more efficient methods that leverage AI capabilities. Provide ongoing training and support for this transformation.

Reskilling and Upskilling:

The pace of AI evolution means that employees need to **continually update their skills**. A workforce without access to ongoing reskilling and upskilling is at risk of falling behind. **Offer opportunities** for employees to reskill and upskill, ensuring they remain relevant and adaptable in the AI-enhanced workplace. This includes regular training and development programs to keep skills up-to-date.

AI-Assisted Work:

Employees may worry that AI will replace them in their roles. Fear of job displacement can lead to resistance to AI adoption. Make it clear that **AI is not about replacing humans but enhancing their capabilities**. Highlight the synergy of human-AI collaboration, where employees work alongside AI to achieve more, rather than being replaced by it.

Feedback and Recognition:

Lack of feedback and recognition can demoralize employees. Without recognition for adapting to AI, **employees may feel undervalued**. Recognize and reward employees who excel in adopting AI-driven processes. Implement feedback mechanisms that encourage ongoing improvement and professional growth.

Building an AI-ready workforce is not a one-time effort but an ongoing process. It involves fostering a culture of AI acceptance, investing in training and development, and ensuring that employees continually adapt to the evolving AI landscape. By doing so, organizations empower their workforce to thrive in an AI-augmented environment and drive operational excellence.

Setting the Right Priorities for AI Integration

Misaligned priorities can lead to inefficient AI implementations and wasted resources. Rushing into AI without a clear strategic plan can result in costly mistakes.

Implementing AI haphazardly can lead to poor ROI and failed initiatives, casting doubt on the value of AI adoption. Without the right priorities, organizations may struggle to leverage AI effectively.

Setting the right priorities for AI integration begins with a strategic plan that aligns AI initiatives with your business goals. Prioritize AI applications that offer the most immediate value and impact. Establish a clear roadmap for AI adoption, addressing areas where AI can make a substantial difference, such as process automation, data analytics, and customer experience enhancement.

Charting Your Course to Excellence

AI integration is a transformative journey, and like any journey, it requires a roadmap with a clear destination. Setting the right priorities for AI integration is the compass that guides your organization toward operational excellence. Here's a deeper look:

Strategic Alignment:

Misaligned priorities can lead to inefficient AI implementations and wasted resources. Rushing into AI without a clear strategic plan can result in costly mistakes. Begin with strategic alignment. Your AI initiatives should align with your overarching business goals. Consider where AI can create the most significant impact, such as process automation, data analytics, and customer experience enhancement.

Immediate Value:

Implementing AI without considering immediate value can lead to poor ROI and failed initiatives. Failed AI initiatives can cast doubt on the value of AI adoption. Prioritize AI applications that offer immediate, tangible value. Start with projects that demonstrate quick wins, gaining buy-in and building confidence in the potential of AI.

Clear Roadmap:

Operating without a clear roadmap can lead to inefficiencies and confusion. A lack of direction can leave employees uncertain about the purpose of AI integration. Develop a clear roadmap for AI adoption that includes defined milestones, timelines, and responsible parties. Ensure that everyone in the organization understands the path forward.

Interdepartmental Collaboration:

Siloed departments can impede the successful integration of AI across the organization. Lack of collaboration can hinder the sharing of valuable data and insights. Encourage interdepartmental collaboration by breaking down silos and promoting communication. AI integration should be a collective effort, involving various departments to maximize its benefits.

Resource Allocation:

Inadequate resource allocation can lead to stalled projects and unfulfilled potential. Insufficient resources can result in missed opportunities and a lack of competitive edge. Allocate the necessary resources, including budgets, personnel, and technology, to support your AI initiatives. Adequate resourcing is vital to ensure successful AI integration.

Measurable Success:

Failing to define and measure success can result in ambiguity and uncertainty. Employees may question the effectiveness of AI if they don't see measurable results. Establish key performance indicators (KPIs) and metrics to measure the success of your AI projects. Regularly evaluate progress and make data-driven adjustments to enhance performance.

Setting the right priorities for AI integration is about creating a clear vision, a strategic plan, and a collaborative environment where everyone understands the value of AI. It's a methodical approach that ensures resources are invested wisely and that the benefits of AI are realized across the organization. By doing so, you can drive operational excellence and maintain a competitive edge in an AI-driven world.

By addressing these three key aspects—making AI adoption a strategic imperative, building an AI-ready workforce, and setting the right priorities for AI integration—organizations can pave the way for successful AI adoption that enhances operational efficiency, decision-making, and innovation while ensuring employees are well-equipped to thrive in the AI-augmented workplace. This chapter sets the foundation for the exciting journey toward workplace excellence powered by AI.

Chapter 7
Success Stories in
Embracing the AI Future

In the ever-evolving landscape of the workplace, embracing the AI future isn't just a matter of staying ahead of the curve; it's a journey toward operational excellence, innovation, and transformative success. As we venture into Chapter 7, we'll take a deep dive into the world of real-life success stories in which organizations have harnessed the power of AI to drive workplace excellence.

These success stories serve as beacons of inspiration and practical insight, showing how AI can bring about profound positive change in various industries and sectors. We'll explore key takeaways and lessons learned from AI trailblazers, shedding light on the strategies and practices that have propelled them to the forefront of innovation and excellence.

This chapter is a testament to the remarkable achievements of organizations that have fully embraced the AI future, providing not just a glimpse into the possibilities but a roadmap for others to follow. Let's embark on a journey through these success stories and uncover the transformative power of AI in the workplace.

Real-Life Case Studies of Workplace Excellence with AI

In this section, we'll explore compelling real-life case studies of organizations that have harnessed the power of AI to achieve workplace excellence. These stories showcase the diversity of industries and applications where AI has made a significant impact. From healthcare to finance, manufacturing to customer service, you'll discover how AI has revolutionized operations, decision-making, and customer experiences.

Key Takeaways and Lessons from AI Trailblazers

Each success story in this section provides valuable lessons and insights into how AI can be effectively implemented. We'll extract key takeaways and lessons learned from these AI trailblazers.

These lessons will encompass:

Strategic Vision: How these organizations developed a clear AI strategy that aligned with their overarching goals.

Data Utilization: The importance of leveraging data to make informed decisions and drive AI initiatives.

Workforce Transformation: The role of reskilling, upskilling, and fostering a culture of continuous learning in preparing the workforce for AI integration.

Customer-Centric Approaches: How AI can enhance customer experiences, drive engagement, and boost satisfaction.

Operational Excellence: Demonstrating how AI has optimized processes, increased efficiency, and reduced costs.

Innovation and Competitive Advantage: How AI has been a catalyst for innovation and helped organizations gain a competitive edge.

Ethical Considerations: Addressing ethical concerns and responsible AI use.

By examining these key takeaways and lessons, you will gain a deep understanding of the principles and practices that underlie successful AI integration. They will be equipped with the knowledge to navigate the complexities of AI adoption in your organization.

"Success Stories in Embracing the AI Future," serves as an inspiring and practical guide to what's possible in the world of AI-driven workplace excellence. As we move forward, you'll be armed with the insights and wisdom gleaned from those who've boldly embraced the AI future and are reaping the rewards of innovation, efficiency, and excellence.

Customer Engagement at Zappos

Zappos, an online shoe and clothing retailer known for its exceptional customer service, has leveraged AI to take customer engagement to new heights. Here's how AI has transformed their approach:

AI-Powered Chatbots: Zappos employs AI-driven chatbots that provide real-time assistance to customers on their website. These chatbots can answer common customer queries, assist in product searches, and even help with order tracking. By doing so, Zappos ensures that customers receive immediate support and guidance, enhancing their overall shopping experience.

<u>Personalized Recommendations</u>: AI algorithms analyze customer behavior and preferences to offer personalized product recommendations. When customers log in, they see tailored suggestions based on their past interactions and purchase history. This not only increases the chances of additional sales but also makes customers feel more valued and understood.

<u>Data-Driven Insights</u>: Zappos uses AI to gather and analyze data from customer interactions. This data helps them identify trends, understand customer needs, and continuously improve their services. AI-driven insights provide a deeper understanding of customer behavior, enabling Zappos to refine its product offerings and marketing strategies.

<u>24/7 Availability</u>: AI-powered chatbots don't have working hours. They are available 24/7, ensuring that customers can receive assistance or answers to their queries at any time. This around-the-clock availability is a testament to Zappos' commitment to customer satisfaction.

Key Takeaways and Lessons from Zappos:

Zappos' success in enhancing customer engagement through AI offers several key takeaways:

<u>Immediate Support</u>: AI-powered chatbots provide immediate responses to customer inquiries, improving the customer experience by reducing response times.

<u>Personalization</u>: Using AI to offer personalized product recommendations demonstrates a deep understanding of customer preferences and fosters customer loyalty.

Data-Driven Insights: Leveraging AI for data analysis allows organizations to better understand and serve their customers by identifying trends and preferences.

24/7 Availability: AI ensures that customer support is available at all times, meeting the expectations of modern consumers who want on-demand service.

Zappos' AI-driven approach to customer engagement serves as a prime example of how organizations can use AI to enhance their operations and build stronger customer relationships, ultimately contributing to workplace excellence.

Retail Revolution with Amazon

Amazon, one of the world's largest e-commerce and technology companies, has been at the forefront of using AI to revolutionize the retail industry. Here are some key examples of how AI has transformed Amazon's operations:

Product Recommendations: Amazon employs sophisticated AI algorithms to offer personalized product recommendations to its customers. When you visit Amazon's website or use its mobile app, you'll see suggestions for products based on your past searches, purchase history, and even products frequently bought together. This personalized approach not only improves the customer experience but also drives sales by increasing the likelihood of additional purchases.

Supply Chain Optimization: AI plays a crucial role in Amazon's supply chain management. Algorithms predict demand for various products, enabling the company to optimize inventory levels and ensure products are in stock when customers need them. This has greatly reduced the risk of stockouts and overstock situations, enhancing customer satisfaction.

Logistics and Delivery: Amazon has been exploring the use of AI-powered drones and autonomous delivery vehicles to expedite its delivery process. AI assists in route optimization, ensuring packages are delivered more efficiently. This innovation not only reduces delivery times but also contributes to cost savings.

Customer Service Chatbots: Amazon uses AI-driven chatbots to assist with customer service inquiries. These chatbots can handle common queries, such as order status and returns, providing quick and efficient support to customers.

Amazon Go Stores: Amazon Go, a chain of convenience stores, employs a unique AI-based system that allows customers to walk in, grab products, and simply walk out without going through a traditional checkout process. Cameras and sensors track what customers take, and they are automatically charged for their selections through their Amazon accounts.

Key Takeaways and Lessons from Amazon:

Amazon's use of AI in the retail industry provides valuable takeaways:

Personalized Customer Experience: AI-driven product recommendations enhance the shopping experience and drive additional sales.

Supply Chain Efficiency: AI helps optimize inventory and ensures products are readily available for customers.

Innovative Delivery Solutions: Amazon's exploration of AI in logistics and delivery shows how technology can improve efficiency and reduce costs.

Efficient Customer Support: AI-driven chatbots offer quick and efficient customer service.

Revolutionary In-Store Experience: Amazon Go stores showcase how AI can transform the in-store shopping experience.

These real-life examples from Amazon underscore the transformative power of AI in enhancing customer engagement and reshaping the retail industry, contributing to operational excellence and innovation.

Manufacturing Efficiency with Siemens' MindSphere

Siemens MindSphere is an industrial IoT (Internet of Things) platform that has been pivotal in optimizing manufacturing operations. Here's how it has revolutionized the manufacturing sector:

Predictive Maintenance: Siemens' MindSphere utilizes sensors and data analytics to monitor machinery and equipment in real-time. It can predict when a machine is likely to fail, allowing manufacturers to perform maintenance proactively. This predictive maintenance not only minimizes costly unplanned downtime but also extends the lifespan of equipment.

Operational Insights: The platform offers deep insights into manufacturing processes by collecting and analyzing data from various points in the production line. Manufacturers can identify inefficiencies, bottlenecks, and areas for improvement, enabling them to enhance overall operational efficiency.

<u>Energy Optimization</u>: MindSphere can monitor energy consumption across manufacturing facilities. This data enables manufacturers to optimize energy usage, reduce costs, and minimize their environmental footprint.

<u>Quality Control</u>: Siemens' platform can identify product defects and deviations from quality standards in real-time. This helps manufacturers maintain high-quality production and reduce waste.

<u>Customization</u>: MindSphere offers the flexibility to create customized applications for specific manufacturing needs. Manufacturers can adapt the platform to suit their unique production processes and requirements.

Key Takeaways and Lessons from Siemens' MindSphere:

Siemens' MindSphere provides several key takeaways:

<u>Predictive Maintenance</u>: AI-driven predictive maintenance can significantly reduce downtime and extend the lifespan of equipment.

<u>Operational Insights</u>: Real-time data analysis provides actionable insights for process optimization.

<u>Energy Efficiency</u>: Monitoring and optimizing energy usage can lead to cost savings and environmental benefits.

<u>Quality Control</u>: AI can enhance product quality and reduce waste.

Customization: The ability to tailor the platform to specific manufacturing needs ensures it's a versatile tool.

Siemens' MindSphere exemplifies how AI and IoT technology can improve manufacturing efficiency, reduce costs, and drive operational excellence, making it a valuable case study for organizations looking to harness the power of AI in their operations.

Key Takeaways and Lessons from AI Trailblazers

These trailblazers offer valuable lessons and takeaways that encompass:

Strategic Vision: The importance of aligning AI initiatives with strategic goals.

Data Utilization: Leveraging data as the lifeblood of AI-driven decision-making.

Workforce Transformation: How reskilling and upskilling are key to preparing employees for AI integration.

Customer-Centric Approaches: Using AI to enhance customer experiences and drive engagement.

Operational Excellence: Demonstrating how AI optimizes processes, increases efficiency, and reduces costs.

Innovation and Competitive Advantage: How AI fuels innovation and creates a competitive edge.

Ethical Considerations: Addressing ethical concerns and responsible AI use.

These real-world examples and lessons serve as practical insights for organizations embarking on their own AI journey, offering a clear roadmap to success and excellence in the age of AI.

Chapter 8
The Path Forward:
Embracing the Future

As we stand on the cusp of the AI-driven future, it's crucial to understand that embracing AI in the workplace is not a destination but an ongoing journey. We will explore the continuous evolution of AI in the workplace and how organizations can prepare for ongoing excellence.

The AI journey is not about reaching a final destination; it's about **continuous growth, adaptability, and transformation**. We'll discuss the importance of embracing AI as a long-term commitment and how organizations can remain at the forefront of innovation, efficiency, and operational excellence.

This chapter serves as a guide to the future, providing insights into how you can prepare your organization to thrive in a world where AI continues to play an increasingly vital role. Together, we'll explore the opportunities, challenges, and strategies that will empower your organization to create a brighter and more successful future with AI.

The Continuous Journey of AI in the Workplace

AI is a dynamic field that's continually evolving. To embrace the future, organizations must acknowledge that their AI journey is an ongoing process. Here's what this section covers:

Adapting to Technological Advances: AI is not static. It continually advances, introducing new capabilities and applications. Organizations should stay updated on the latest AI trends and technologies to remain competitive.

Integration and Optimization: As AI evolves, organizations need to integrate new AI solutions and continuously optimize their existing ones. This might involve refining algorithms, expanding data sources, or enhancing AI-driven processes.

Ethical Considerations: The ethical use of AI is a paramount concern. Organizations must stay vigilant in ensuring that AI is used responsibly, respecting privacy, fairness, and transparency.

Data-Driven Decision-Making: A data-centric approach should be embedded in the organization's culture. The continuous journey involves collecting and analyzing data to drive informed decisions.

Preparing for Ongoing Excellence with AI

Excellence with AI is not a one-time achievement but a commitment to continuous improvement. This section addresses:

Reskilling and Upskilling: The **workforce must be equipped to adapt to evolving AI technologies**. Regular reskilling and upskilling initiatives are vital to ensure that employees can leverage AI effectively.

Innovation Culture: Fostering a culture of innovation is essential. **Encourage employees to suggest and implement AI-driven solutions** that can enhance processes, products, or services.

Strategic Partnerships: Collaboration with AI experts, startups, and industry peers can provide access to cutting-edge technology and expertise. Establishing strategic partnerships can be a **crucial part of your ongoing journey**.

Transforming Your Organization for a Brighter Future

The path forward involves the transformation of the organization as a whole. Here's what this section covers:

Agile Leadership: Leadership should be **adaptable and responsive to changes** in the AI landscape. Agile leadership can guide the organization toward a brighter future.

Change Management: Effectively managing change is a key factor in the ongoing success of AI integration. Organizations must **create change management strategies** that help employees embrace and adapt to new AI-driven processes.

Customer-Centric Approach: AI can **enhance customer experiences**. Organizations should continue to focus on a customer-centric approach, using AI to provide better service and meet evolving customer expectations.

Sustainability and Responsibility: The future of AI integration includes a **focus on sustainability and social responsibility**. Organizations should ensure their AI initiatives align with these principles, benefiting both the organization and society.

A Brighter Future with AI

We emphasize that the future is bright for organizations that embrace the ongoing journey of AI in the workplace. By adapting to technological advances, preparing for ongoing excellence, and transforming the organization, you are positioning yourself for a future where AI is a powerful ally in achieving operational excellence and innovation.

Remember that the path forward with AI is not a linear one; it's a dynamic journey filled with opportunities for growth, improvement, and success. By **continually embracing AI,** your organization can look forward to a future that is brighter, more efficient, and filled with new possibilities. The key to success is not just in embracing AI but in persistently adapting and evolving with it.

Building a Future of Innovation and Excellence

Agile Leadership: The successful integration of AI requires leadership that is not only visionary but also agile. Leaders must be **open to change** and responsive to the rapidly evolving AI landscape. They should **encourage experimentation**, learning from failures, and adapting strategies based on real-time insights. Agile leadership fosters an environment where AI initiatives can thrive and where leaders lead by example in embracing new technologies and approaches.

<u>Change Management</u>: Effectively **managing change is critical** when introducing AI into an organization. The adoption of AI often **involves significant shifts in processes, roles, and responsibilities**. A structured change management strategy is necessary to guide employees through these transitions. It includes communication plans, training programs, and support systems to ensure that employees understand the changes and feel comfortable with them.

<u>Employee Involvement and Empowerment</u>: Organizations that are successful in AI transformation actively **involve and empower their employees**. They create a culture where employees are encouraged to provide input and participate in the decision-making process regarding AI initiatives. Employees on the front lines often have **valuable insights into how AI can improve processes and customer experiences**. Empowering them to innovate with AI can yield substantial benefits.

<u>Customer-Centric Approach</u>: One of the primary goals of AI integration is to enhance the customer experience. Organizations should **prioritize a customer-centric approach** to their AI initiatives. AI can be used to gain deeper insights into customer behavior, predict needs, and personalize interactions. Ensuring that AI aligns with customers' expectations and provides value is essential for long-term success.

<u>Ethical AI Use and Responsibility</u>: AI brings with it ethical considerations that organizations must address. Responsible AI use involves ensuring fairness, transparency, and accountability in AI systems. Organizations should e**stablish ethical guidelines and practices that guide the development and deployment of AI solutions**. This not only safeguards against ethical dilemmas but also builds trust among customers, employees, and stakeholders.

<u>Sustainability and Social Responsibility</u>: As organizations transform through AI, they should consider the broader implications of their actions. This includes assessing the environmental impact of AI operations and promoting sustainability. Furthermore, organizations have a role to play in **addressing societal challenges through AI**. For instance, AI can be used to create solutions for healthcare, education, environmental conservation, and other areas that benefit society as a whole.

<u>Continuous Learning and Adaptation</u>: AI is a field that is constantly evolving. Organizations must foster a culture of continuous learning and adaptation. This involves staying updated on the latest AI trends, technologies, and best practices. It also means **investing in ongoing education and training programs for employees**, ensuring they are well-prepared for the ever-changing AI landscape.

<u>Collaboration and Partnerships</u>: Successful transformation often **involves collaborations and partnerships with AI experts, startups, research institutions, and industry peers**. These collaborations provide access to cutting-edge technology and expertise, enabling organizations to remain at the forefront of AI innovation.

Transforming an organization for AI is a multifaceted process that involves agile leadership, change management, employee involvement, a customer-centric approach, ethical considerations, sustainability, continuous learning, and strategic collaborations. Organizations that actively embrace these elements can create a future of innovation, efficiency, and excellence powered by AI.

Chapter 9
Reskilling and Upskilling for the AI Era

Preparing Your Workforce for AI Excellence

In this rapidly changing landscape, reskilling and upskilling have become essential strategies for organizations seeking to thrive in the AI era. This chapter explores the significance of these initiatives and outlines the steps required to empower your workforce with the knowledge and skills needed for AI integration.

Reskilling and Upskilling Defined

Reskilling and upskilling are not just buzzwords; they are vital components of a forward-thinking organization. This section provides clear definitions and distinctions between the two:

> Reskilling: The process of **training employees in new skills** or roles to adapt to changing job requirements, often as a response to evolving technologies.

<u>Upskilling</u>: The act of **teaching employees new skills** that are relevant to their current roles, often aimed at enhancing their proficiency and employability.

Why Reskilling and Upskilling are Vital in the AI Era

This section dives into the crucial role of reskilling and upskilling in the AI-driven workplace:

<u>Fostering Adaptability:</u> AI integration brings changes to job roles and tasks. Reskilling **empowers employees to adapt and take on new responsibilities**.

<u>Enhancing Efficiency</u>: Upskilling **improves employees' proficiency,** making them more productive and efficient in their roles.

<u>Addressing Skill Gaps</u>: The evolving AI landscape **often reveals skill gaps**. Reskilling and upskilling help bridge these gaps to ensure the workforce remains competitive.

<u>Boosting Innovation</u>: A workforce equipped with the latest skills is better positioned to innovate and contribute to the organization's **growth and competitiveness**.

Steps to Effective Reskilling and Upskilling

Reskilling and upskilling require a structured approach. This section outlines a step-by-step guide to implementing effective reskilling and upskilling programs:

Skills Assessment: Identify the current skills of your workforce and areas that need improvement.

Strategic Planning: Develop a reskilling and upskilling strategy aligned with the organization's goals and the evolving needs of your industry.

Curriculum Design: Create training programs that focus on the specific skills and knowledge required.

Engagement and Participation: Encourage employees to actively participate in reskilling and upskilling initiatives.

Continuous Learning Culture: Foster a culture where learning is ongoing and employees are encouraged to develop new skills.

Mentoring and Coaching: Implement mentoring programs to support employees in their learning journey.

Evaluation and Feedback: Continuously assess the effectiveness of reskilling and upskilling programs and gather feedback from participants.

The Importance of Patience in the Process

Reskilling and upskilling are not quick fixes; they are ongoing processes that require patience. This section highlights the importance of patience in seeing the long-term benefits of these initiatives:

Varied Learning Paces: Employees learn at different speeds, and it's crucial to accommodate this variety.

<u>Trial and Error:</u> Reskilling and upskilling may involve some trial and error. Not all approaches will yield immediate results, and that's okay.

<u>Long-Term Vision:</u> Keep your eye on the long-term vision, understanding that the benefits of reskilling and upskilling may take time to manifest fully.

Nurturing Talent for AI Excellence

It's clear that reskilling and upskilling are not just investments in employees; they are investments in the future of your organization. In the AI era, nurturing talent and providing continuous opportunities for learning are the keys to achieving operational excellence and innovation. Patience and a commitment to ongoing growth will ensure that your workforce remains prepared for the evolving landscape of the AI-driven workplace.

Chapter 10
Ethical Considerations in
AI Integration

The Ethical Landscape of AI

In a world increasingly powered by artificial intelligence, ethical considerations are paramount. As organizations integrate AI into their operations, a profound responsibility emerges: ensuring that AI technologies are used in a manner that upholds ethical principles and aligns with societal values. This chapter delves into the complex and vital realm of ethical considerations in AI integration.

AI and Ethical Dilemmas

The rise of AI brings with it a range of ethical dilemmas. This section discusses some of the most pressing concerns:

Bias and Fairness: AI algorithms can perpetuate biases present in historical data. We explore the challenges of ensuring fairness in AI systems and strategies to mitigate bias.

Transparency: The "black box" nature of AI can make it challenging to understand how decisions are made. We delve into the importance of transparency in AI processes and how to achieve it.

Privacy: AI often relies on vast amounts of personal data. This section discusses the ethical implications of data privacy and strategies for responsible data handling.

Accountability: When AI systems make decisions, who is accountable for their outcomes? We address the need for clear lines of accountability and the role of organizations and individuals in AI responsibility.

Navigating the Complex Terrain

In the age of AI, organizations face a multitude of ethical challenges that demand careful consideration. Here are some key ethical dilemmas associated with AI integration:

Bias and Fairness: AI systems often learn from historical data, which can contain biases. When these biases are perpetuated in AI algorithms, it can lead to discriminatory outcomes. Ethical dilemmas arise in ensuring fairness and equity, especially when AI systems impact decisions related to employment, lending, or criminal justice.

Transparency: The inherent complexity of AI algorithms can create opacity in decision-making processes, resulting in a lack of transparency. Ethical concerns arise when individuals cannot understand how or why certain AI-driven decisions are made, particularly when they affect their lives or rights.

Privacy: AI often relies on vast amounts of personal data. Ethical dilemmas emerge in the responsible collection and use of this data. Maintaining privacy and obtaining informed consent from individuals whose data is processed is crucial.

Accountability: When AI systems make decisions, it can be challenging to determine who is accountable for the outcomes. Establishing clear lines of accountability is an ethical dilemma, especially when AI-driven decisions have real-world consequences.

Job Displacement: The fear of AI displacing human workers is a prominent ethical concern. Organizations must navigate the dilemma of automating tasks for efficiency while ensuring displaced workers have access to reskilling and upskilling opportunities.

Mitigating Ethical Dilemmas in AI Integration

To address these ethical dilemmas, organizations must implement ethical practices in their AI integration efforts:

Ethics by Design: Incorporating ethics at the design stage of AI projects ensures that ethical considerations are embedded in the technology from the outset.

Ethics Committees: Many organizations establish ethics committees or advisory boards to oversee AI projects. These committees guide ethical issues and evaluate AI initiatives from an ethical perspective.

<u>AI Auditing</u>: Regular audits of AI systems help identify and rectify ethical concerns. This practice involves evaluating AI systems for bias, transparency, and fairness.

<u>Continuous Ethics Education</u>: Providing ongoing ethics education and training to employees involved in AI projects ensures that they understand the ethical implications of their work.

The Ongoing Ethical Journey

Ethical considerations in AI integration are an ongoing journey. As AI technologies and applications evolve, so do the associated ethical dilemmas. Organizations must continuously adapt their practices to address new ethical challenges that emerge.

Ethics in AI is not only a compliance requirement but also a fundamental ethical duty. Responsible AI use is essential for building trust with customers, employees, and the broader community. It involves a commitment to using AI technologies in ways that benefit both organizations and society at large, aligning with the principles of fairness, transparency, privacy, and accountability.

Building Ethical AI Practices

This section provides insights into fostering ethical AI integration within organizations:

Ethics by Design: Emphasizing the concept of "ethics by design," we discuss the importance of considering ethics at the outset of AI development.

Ethics Committees: Many organizations establish ethics committees or advisory boards to oversee AI projects. We explore their role and impact on ethical AI practices.

AI Auditing: The practice of auditing AI systems for ethical compliance is examined, including best practices for conducting such audits.

Continuous Ethics Education: We stress the importance of providing continuous ethics education and training to employees involved in AI projects.

A Foundation for Responsible Integration

The responsible integration of AI into organizations is contingent on the establishment of robust ethical practices. Building ethical AI practices not only ensures compliance with regulatory requirements but also fosters trust among stakeholders, including employees, customers, and the broader community. Here are key elements of building ethical AI practices:

Ethics by Design: Putting Ethics at the Core

Ethics by design is a foundational principle that advocates for considering ethical implications at the inception of AI projects. This approach emphasizes **embedding ethical considerations into the development process, from data collection to algorithm design**.

Data Ethics: Ethical AI practices commence with responsible data collection. Organizations must ensure that data used in AI models is ethically sourced, representative, and free from biases. This may involve data anonymization, consent mechanisms, and data governance frameworks.

Algorithmic Transparency: Ethical AI design prioritizes algorithmic transparency. This entails creating AI models and systems that provide explanations for their decisions, enabling users to understand the reasoning behind AI-driven outcomes.

Fairness and Equity: Addressing bias is a fundamental ethical concern. Ethical AI practices include measures to identify, mitigate, and prevent biases in AI algorithms to ensure fairness and equity in decision-making.

Ethics Committees: Oversight and Guidance.....Many organizations establish ethics committees or advisory boards dedicated to overseeing AI projects. These committees comprise experts in ethics, technology, and relevant domains. Their role is to provide guidance on ethical matters, evaluate AI initiatives from an ethical perspective, and advise on mitigating potential ethical dilemmas.

Ethical Impact Assessment: Ethics committees may conduct ethical impact assessments of AI projects, identifying risks, ethical concerns, and potential consequences. They provide recommendations for addressing these issues.

Policy Development: Ethics committees contribute to the development of ethical policies and guidelines that inform AI practices within the organization. These policies set the ethical framework for AI projects.

AI Auditing: Ensuring Ethical Compliance

Regular AI auditing is essential for ensuring that AI systems and practices align with ethical standards. **Auditing involves evaluating AI models, algorithms, and data-handling processes for ethical compliance**.

> Bias Audits: One critical aspect of AI auditing is bias assessment. Audits are conducted to identify, measure, and address bias in AI algorithms to ensure fairness and equity.

> Transparency Audits: Audits also examine algorithmic transparency, assessing the extent to which AI systems provide explanations for their decisions. Transparency audits aim to make AI decision-making more understandable and interpretable.

Continuous Ethics Education: Fostering Ethical Awareness

Employees involved in AI projects need to be aware of the ethical implications of their work. Organizations should provide continuous ethics education and training to ensure that employees **understand the ethical considerations relevant to their roles**.

> Ethics Workshops: Conducting ethics workshops and training sessions that cover topics such as bias mitigation,

data privacy, and transparency can enhance employees' ethical awareness.

<u>Ethical Decision-Making</u>: Education should focus on equipping employees with the skills to make ethical decisions in the context of AI projects. This includes recognizing ethical dilemmas and knowing how to address them.

Building ethical AI practices is a multifaceted endeavor that encompasses ethics by design, oversight through ethics committees, regular auditing for ethical compliance, and the cultivation of a culture of ethical awareness. These practices align AI initiatives with ethical principles and contribute to building trust and credibility for organizations in an AI-driven world. Ethical AI isn't a one-time task; it's a continuous commitment to upholding ethical standards in the ever-evolving AI landscape.

Fostering ethical awareness is not just a recommendation; it's an imperative. We believe in integrating this core value not only into our job descriptions but also into our Employee Value Proposition (EVP). Your commitment to ethical awareness goes beyond words; it's woven into the very fabric of our organization.

When candidates read a job description and are hired, they are not only embracing a role; they are joining a culture that prioritizes integrity, responsibility, and a deep ethical understanding as part of the job description.

Your EVP extends this commitment by offering you an environment where your ethical values align with your professional growth. We see ethical awareness as a cornerstone of excellence, and we invite you to be a part of this culture, where your values, and our organizational values, align seamlessly.

Here are some things to consider when incorporating ethical awareness into job descriptions and the Employee Value Proposition (EVP):

Align with Company Values: Ensure that the ethical expectations outlined in job descriptions and the EVP align with the company's core values and principles. This consistency demonstrates a commitment to ethics throughout the organization.

Be Specific: Specify the ethical behaviors and standards expected from employees. Use concrete examples to illustrate ethical responsibilities, making it clear what ethical awareness entails in the context of the role.

Highlight Ethical Leadership: Emphasize that ethical awareness is not just for individual contributors but is also a critical trait for leaders and managers. Showcase the company's commitment to ethical leadership.

Provide Training: Mention any training or development opportunities related to ethical awareness. This can include ethics training, ongoing education, or access to resources that help employees understand and address ethical issues.

Integrate into EVP: Ensure that ethical awareness is integrated into the organization's

Employee Value Proposition. Highlight how embracing ethics in the workplace contributes to a positive work environment, personal growth, and long-term career satisfaction.

Demonstrate Accountability: Make it clear that ethical lapses will be addressed seriously and swiftly. This demonstrates the organization's commitment to maintaining high ethical standards.

Encourage Reporting: Communicate the procedures for reporting ethical concerns and encourage employees to speak up without fear of retaliation. Show how the organization supports and protects whistleblowers.

Cultivate Ethical Culture: Describe how the organization actively fosters an ethical culture and encourages employees to be ethical ambassadors both inside and outside the workplace.

Showcase Impact: Illustrate how ethical awareness positively impacts the organization, its clients, and the community. Highlight real-world examples of how ethical practices have made a difference.

Regular Review: Regularly review and update job descriptions and EVP to ensure they reflect the evolving ethical landscape and organizational goals.

Leadership Commitment: Demonstrate leadership's commitment to ethical awareness, showcasing that it starts at the top and permeates throughout the organization.

By considering these points, organizations can effectively incorporate ethical awareness into job descriptions and the EVP, creating a workplace culture that values and prioritizes ethics.

The Road Ahead: Ethical AI Integration

We emphasize that ethical considerations in AI integration are an ongoing journey. Organizations must **continuously adapt** to the **evolving ethical landscape of AI**. As they do so, they not only fulfill their ethical responsibilities but also build trust with customers, employees, and the broader community.

This serves as a foundation for understanding the **critical importance of ethical considerations** in AI integration. It offers guidance on **navigating the complex ethical landscape and underscores** that responsible AI use is not just a compliance requirement but a fundamental ethical duty.

As you adopt AI technologies, the road ahead is marked by a continuous commitment to ethical AI integration. Navigating the evolving ethical landscape in AI is essential for building trust and ensuring responsible AI use. Here are some key considerations for the path forward:

Continuous Ethical Adaptation: Ethical considerations in AI integration are not static. They evolve alongside technology and societal expectations. Organizations must remain agile and **adapt to emerging ethical challenges**. This requires a commitment to ongoing ethical assessments and adjustments.

Public Engagement: Ethical AI integration should involve stakeholders beyond the organization, including customers, users, and the broader community. Public engagement enables organizations to **understand diverse perspectives and concerns, fostering transparency and accountability**.

Regulatory Compliance: Compliance with legal and regulatory frameworks is fundamental to ethical AI integration. Organizations must stay informed about evolving AI-related legislation and ensure their AI practices adhere to these regulations.

Ethical AI Champions: Appointing internal champions for ethical AI practices can be instrumental. These individuals or teams are responsible for **advocating ethical considerations and driving compliance within the organization.**

Transparency Initiatives: Promoting transparency in AI systems is not only an ethical obligation but also a way to build trust. Organizations should **implement transparency initiatives**, such as disclosing data sources, algorithms, and decision-making processes to users and stakeholders.

Education and Awareness: Building ethical AI integration requires ongoing education and awareness efforts. Employees involved in AI projects should **receive training to recognize and address ethical dilemmas**. Organizations can also engage in public awareness campaigns about their AI practices.

Stakeholder Feedback Mechanisms: Establishing mechanisms for stakeholders to provide feedback on AI-related practices and outcomes is vital. This feedback loop can **inform adjustments and improvements in ethical AI integration.**

Responsible Data Governance: Ethical AI integration is closely linked to data governance. Organizations should **ensure responsible data collection**, handling, and usage, including obtaining informed consent and protecting privacy.

Third-Party Audits: Independent audits of AI systems by third-party organizations or experts can provide an objective assessment of ethical compliance. These audits contribute to **transparency and trust-building.**

Ethical Leadership: Ethical AI integration starts at the top. Leadership should **set the tone** for ethical practices and demonstrate a commitment to responsible AI use.

Ethical AI integration is an ongoing journey, not a destination. Organizations must traverse the evolving landscape of AI ethics with adaptability, transparency, and a commitment to societal well-being. By actively engaging with stakeholders, staying informed about regulations, and continuously improving their ethical AI practices, organizations can build trust and credibility in the AI era, fostering a harmonious relationship between AI technologies and humanity.

Chapter 11
AI in Supply Chain and Logistics

The Transformation of Supply Chain and Logistics

In an era marked by unprecedented technological advancements, the integration of artificial intelligence has revolutionized supply chain and logistics operations. Explores the profound impact of AI on these critical sectors, from **enhancing demand forecasting to optimizing routes and managing inventories**. AI-driven innovations are reshaping the way organizations manage and streamline their supply chains, resulting in remarkable gains in efficiency and competitiveness.

The Power of AI in Demand Forecasting

Precision Forecasting: AI-powered demand forecasting leverages vast datasets, real-time information, and advanced predictive analytics to **provide organizations with highly accurate demand predictions**. This section delves into how AI improves forecasting accuracy, leading to reduced stockouts, overstock, and improved customer satisfaction.

<u>Dynamic Demand Management:</u> AI enables organizations to respond dynamically to fluctuations in demand. We discuss how **AI algorithms can adjust inventory levels and supply chain processes in real-time**, ensuring products are available when and where they're needed.

Route Optimization and Transportation Efficiency

<u>Route Planning</u>: AI systems optimize transportation routes for **cost-efficiency and timely deliveries**. This section explores how AI considers factors like traffic conditions, weather, and vehicle constraints to create the most efficient routes.

<u>Fleet Management</u>: AI assists in fleet management by monitoring vehicle health, **optimizing maintenance schedules, and improving fuel efficiency**. This part of the chapter discusses the tangible benefits of AI in reducing operational costs and increasing vehicle longevity.

Revolutionizing Inventory Management

<u>Inventory Optimization</u>: AI-driven inventory management minimizes holding costs while maintaining optimal stock levels. The chapter explains how organizations use AI to prevent overstock and understock situations, freeing up capital and enhancing operational agility.

<u>Predictive Maintenance:</u> AI enables predictive maintenance in supply chain machinery and vehicles. We discuss how AI systems

monitor equipment conditions and provide early warnings of potential failures, reducing downtime and repair costs.

AI and the Supply Chain of the Future

Blockchain and Transparency: AI combined with blockchain technology enhances supply chain transparency and traceability. This section explores how organizations use AI to track products from origin to destination, addressing issues like product recalls and counterfeit goods.

Sustainability: AI-driven supply chain management takes environmental and sustainability factors into account. We discuss how AI can optimize routes to reduce emissions and minimize the carbon footprint of supply chain operations.

Case Studies in AI-Enhanced Supply Chain

The chapter includes real-world case studies showcasing how organizations have successfully integrated AI into their supply chain and logistics operations. These examples highlight the quantifiable benefits of AI, such as cost savings, improved customer satisfaction, and enhanced operational efficiency.

Nestlé's AI-Enhanced Transparency

Nestlé, a food and beverage company, implemented AI and blockchain technology to enhance supply chain transparency. Customers can now scan QR codes on Nestlé products to access information about the product's journey, including sourcing and production details. This initiative improved customer trust and enabled Nestlé to address quality concerns more effectively.

These case studies highlight the real-world application of AI in supply chain and logistics, demonstrating how organizations across various industries leverage AI to optimize operations, reduce costs, improve efficiency, and enhance transparency and sustainability in their supply chain practices.

Walmart's AI-Enhanced Inventory Management

Walmart, a leading retailer, integrated AI into its inventory management processes. AI-driven systems analyze sales data, seasonal trends, and supplier performance to optimize inventory levels. This approach resulted in a 30% reduction in overstock situations and a 25% reduction in holding costs. Walmart's AI-powered inventory management enhances customer satisfaction while improving operational efficiency.

DHL's AI-Powered Route Optimization

DHL, a global logistics company, utilized AI to optimize its delivery routes. By considering factors such as traffic conditions, weather, and delivery windows, DHL improved route planning and reduced delivery times. This optimization led to a 15% reduction in transportation costs and a 20% decrease in carbon emissions. DHL's use of AI not only increased efficiency but also aligned with sustainability goals.

The AI-Driven Future of Supply Chain and Logistics

In closing, the chapter emphasizes that AI is not merely a buzzword in supply chain and logistics; it is the driving force behind transformative change. As organizations continue to invest in AI technologies, they are poised to reap the rewards of enhanced demand forecasting, optimized routes, efficient inventory management, and sustainability. The supply chain and logistics landscape is undergoing a fundamental shift, and AI is at the forefront of this revolution, shaping a future marked by efficiency, precision, and competitiveness.

Chapter 12
How AI is Transforming
Decision-Making

The Decisive Impact of AI

In the modern business landscape, AI is ushering in a new era of decision-making. This chapter delves into how AI technologies are **influencing decision-making processes** across various industries, from enhancing data analytics to providing predictive decision support. The transformation brought about by AI **isn't limited to tactical choices; it extends to strategic and operational decisions that shape the future of organizations.**

AI-Powered Data Analytics

> Advanced-Data Insights: AI-driven analytics processes vast datasets at unprecedented speeds, uncovering deep insights and patterns. This section explores how AI enables organizations to make data-informed decisions, from market trends to customer behavior.

> Predictive Analytics: AI isn't limited to historical data analysis. It predicts future outcomes by utilizing machine learning algorithms

to recognize patterns and trends. We discuss how predictive analytics empowers organizations to make proactive decisions, minimizing risks and maximizing opportunities.

AI in Decision Support

Predictive Decision Support Systems: AI-powered decision support systems assist organizations in making complex, data-driven decisions. This part of the chapter illustrates how these systems provide actionable insights, enabling informed choices in areas like finance, healthcare, and manufacturing.

Cognitive Decision Support: AI technologies equipped with natural language processing (NLP) and machine learning help decision-makers extract valuable information from unstructured data sources. We explore how cognitive decision support systems improve knowledge management and decision-making across diverse sectors.

Cognitive Decision Support: Augmenting Human Intelligence

Cognitive Decision Support is an advanced application of artificial intelligence (AI) that empowers organizations to **extract valuable insights** from unstructured data sources and, in turn, enhances decision-making processes. Unlike traditional decision support systems that rely primarily on structured data and predefined rules, cognitive decision support leverages natural language processing (NLP), machine learning, and other AI techniques to handle complex and unstructured information.

Key Aspects of Cognitive Decision Support:

Natural Language Processing (NLP): NLP is a **fundamental component of cognitive decision support.** It enables systems to understand and process human language, making it possible to analyze unstructured text, such as emails, reports, social media content, and customer feedback. NLP allows organizations to **gain insights** from this wealth of textual information, uncovering trends, sentiments, and valuable knowledge.

Machine Learning Algorithms: Cognitive decision support systems employ machine learning algorithms to **identify patterns**, associations, and anomalies within unstructured data. By continuously learning from the data, these systems become more accurate and efficient over time, offering organizations the ability to **make more informed decisions**.

Applications of Cognitive Decision Support:

Customer Feedback Analysis: Organizations can use cognitive decision support to analyze customer feedback and reviews from various sources. By extracting sentiments and identifying common issues or concerns, companies can make data-driven improvements to their products and services, ultimately **enhancing customer satisfaction**.

Knowledge Management: Cognitive decision support systems assist in managing vast repositories of unstructured data, such as internal documents, research papers, and historical records. They

enable employees to access relevant information quickly, fostering knowledge sharing and **efficient decision-making**.

Risk Assessment and Compliance: In industries like finance and healthcare, cognitive decision support aids in risk assessment and regulatory compliance. By analyzing unstructured data sources, such as legal documents or medical records, these systems can **identify potential risks** and ensure organizations adhere to industry regulations.

Market Research: Cognitive decision support plays a crucial role in market research by analyzing text data from social media, news articles, and market reports. This allows organizations to **gain insights into market trends**, consumer preferences, and competitive intelligence, shaping their strategic decisions.

Benefits of Cognitive Decision Support:

Enhanced Decision Quality: Cognitive decision support provides decision-makers with **deeper insights**, enabling them to **make more informed and contextually relevant decisions**.

Efficiency and Productivity: By automating the analysis of unstructured data, cognitive decision support systems save time and effort, **making information more readily available** to support decision-making processes.

Competitive Advantage: Organizations that leverage cognitive decision support **gain a competitive edge** by staying ahead of market trends, understanding customer sentiments, and responding rapidly to emerging opportunities or challenges.

In summary, cognitive decision support is a vital tool for organizations seeking to harness the power of unstructured data. It not only augments human intelligence by providing deeper insights but also enhances the efficiency and productivity of decision-making processes. This technology plays a pivotal role in modern data-driven decision-making across various industries.

Strategic Decision-Making with AI

AI in Strategy Formulation:* AI aids in strategic decision-making by identifying market opportunities, potential threats, and competitive advantages. We discuss how AI supports organizations in developing more informed, dynamic, and agile strategies.

Revolutionizing Decision-Making

AI in strategy formulation represents a significant shift in the way organizations plan for the future. It leverages artificial intelligence and machine learning to provide data-driven insights that inform strategic decisions. This transformative approach to strategy development empowers organizations to create more informed, dynamic, and agile strategies.

Key Aspects of AI in Strategy Formulation:

<u>Data-Driven Insights</u>: AI processes vast amounts of data, both structured and unstructured, to provide organizations with a **comprehensive understanding of their market, competition, and internal operations**. By analyzing historical data and real-time information, AI identifies patterns, trends, and anomalies that humans may overlook.

<u>Market Analysis</u>: AI assists in market analysis by examining market trends, consumer behavior, and competitive landscapes. It enables organizations to **identify emerging opportunities and potential threats**, allowing for proactive strategy adjustments.

<u>Competitive Intelligence</u>: AI keeps organizations **informed about the actions and strategies of their competitors**. It continuously monitors competitors' activities, helping organizations stay ahead in the market and respond to changing dynamics effectively.

Benefits of AI in Strategy Formulation:

<u>Enhanced Precision</u>: AI eliminates the guesswork in strategy formulation by providing precise, data-backed insights. Organizations can **develop strategies** based on real-time, **accurate information**.

<u>Agility and Adaptability</u>: AI allows organizations to be agile and adaptive in their strategy development. They can quickly **adjust strategies in response to changing market conditions, emerging trends, or unexpected disruptions**.

<u>Risk Mitigation:</u> AI helps in identifying potential risks and challenges in advance. By analyzing data and trends, organizations can proactively **plan strategies to mitigate risks** and capitalize on opportunities.

<u>Improved Resource Allocation</u>: AI optimizes resource allocation by **identifying areas of growth and efficiency**. It ensures that resources, such as budget, personnel, and technology, are deployed effectively in alignment with strategic objectives.

Real-World Applications of AI in Strategy Formulation:

<u>Retail Industry</u>: Retailers use AI to analyze customer purchasing behavior and market trends, leading to informed decisions about product selection, pricing, and inventory management.

<u>Healthcare</u>: Healthcare organizations utilize AI to develop strategies for patient care, resource allocation, and disease management. AI helps in predictive modeling for disease outbreaks and resource planning.

<u>Finance</u>: Financial institutions employ AI to create investment strategies, portfolio management, and risk assessment. AI aids in identifying investment opportunities and optimizing financial decisions.

AI in strategy formulation is a game-changer for organizations across industries. By providing data-driven insights, enhancing precision, and promoting agility, AI empowers organizations to make informed, dynamic, and resilient strategic decisions. As technology continues to evolve, it will play an increasingly central role in shaping the strategies that define the future of organizations.

Operational Decision Transformation:

AI doesn't just influence high-level strategic decisions; it **transforms operational choices** as well. Organizations can optimize production processes, allocate resources, and manage logistics more efficiently with AI.

Harnessing AI for Efficiency

Operational decision transformation represents the adaptation of artificial intelligence (AI) to optimize everyday choices in an organization's operations. While strategic decisions define the overarching direction of a company, operational decisions involve the day-to-day choices that determine how efficiently and effectively those strategies are executed. **AI plays a crucial role in streamlining and enhancing these operational decisions**.

Key Aspects of Operational Decision Transformation:

Production Process Optimization: AI assists organizations in optimizing their production processes. By analyzing real-time data from machinery, AI can identify inefficiencies, reduce downtime, and improve the overall productivity of the production line.

Resource Allocation: Operational decisions often revolve around resource allocation. AI helps organizations allocate resources like personnel, inventory, and equipment efficiently, ensuring that the right resources are available at the right time and place.

Logistics and Supply Chain Management: AI is invaluable in making operational decisions related to logistics and supply chain. It optimizes route planning, reduces transportation costs, and minimizes delays in the delivery of goods.

Customer Service and Support: AI-powered chatbots and virtual assistants are revolutionizing operational decisions in customer service. They handle routine inquiries, providing rapid responses and freeing up human agents for more complex and strategic tasks.

Benefits of Operational Decision Transformation:

Cost Efficiency: AI-driven operational decisions often lead to cost savings. By optimizing processes and resource allocation, organizations reduce operational expenses and improve profitability.

Enhanced Productivity: AI streamlines operational decisions, increasing productivity and reducing manual intervention. This frees up employees to focus on tasks that require human creativity and problem-solving.

Faster Response Times: AI enables rapid and data-driven decision-making, especially in areas like logistics and customer service. This leads to quicker response times, improving customer satisfaction and overall efficiency.

Reduced Human Error: Operational decisions can be susceptible to human error. AI, with its precision and consistency, minimizes errors and enhances decision quality.

Real-World Applications of Operational Decision Transformation:

Manufacturing: Manufacturers use AI to optimize production schedules, predict maintenance needs, and enhance quality control. These operational decisions result in streamlined manufacturing processes and cost savings.

E-commerce: In e-commerce, AI-driven recommendations and inventory management decisions lead to improved customer experiences and more efficient supply chain operations.

<u>Healthcare</u>: Healthcare providers rely on AI for patient scheduling, resource allocation, and optimizing hospital operations. AI helps ensure that patients receive timely care, reducing waiting times and improving healthcare outcomes.

Operational decision transformation, powered by AI, is a pivotal aspect of ensuring an organization's efficiency and effectiveness in its day-to-day operations. By applying AI to these operational decisions, organizations can achieve cost savings, enhance productivity, and provide better service to customers, ultimately contributing to overall success and competitiveness.

Unleashing Efficiency with AI in Operational Decisions

In the ever-evolving landscape of business and industry, operational decision transformation emerges as a driving force that leverages the power of artificial intelligence (AI) to revolutionize the daily choices that shape organizations. From optimizing production processes to refining logistics and resource allocation, **AI empowers operational decision-makers with unparalleled precision and efficiency**.

The benefits of operational decision transformation are manifest. AI-driven operational decisions lead to cost efficiency, enhanced productivity, faster response times, and a reduction in human error. These advantages ripple throughout an organization, **positively impacting its bottom line**, customer satisfaction, and competitive edge.

In the manufacturing sector, **AI fine-tunes production schedules and quality control, ensuring that products are delivered on time and with superior quality**. In the realm of e-commerce, AI recommendations and inventory management decisions create personalized and efficient shopping experiences. Healthcare providers benefit from AI-powered operational decisions by **optimizing patient scheduling and resource allocation**, resulting in prompt and effective healthcare delivery.

As we move forward, it is clear that the integration of AI in operational decision-making is not a mere trend but a transformative evolution. Organizations that embrace AI-driven operational decisions are **well-positioned to streamline processes, reduce costs, and ultimately enhance their competitiveness**. The AI-powered operational decision transformation represents the path to a more efficient, productive, and responsive future, where organizations can meet the demands of a rapidly changing world with confidence and agility.

The Lexicon of Strategic AI: A Comprehensive Glossary

AI (Artificial Intelligence): The development of computer systems that can perform tasks that typically require human intelligence, such as learning, reasoning, problem-solving, and decision-making.

Operational Transformation: Optimizing daily operational decisions and processes within an organization to enhance efficiency and productivity.

Digital Transformation: The integration of digital technologies into various aspects of an organization, fundamentally changing how it operates and delivers value to customers.

Strategy Formulation: The process of creating and implementing strategies to achieve organizational goals and objectives.

Decision-Making: The process of selecting a course of action or choice from available alternatives to achieve specific goals or solve problems.

Cognitive Decision Support: AI-driven systems that assist decision-makers in extracting valuable insights from unstructured data sources, enhancing knowledge management and decision-making.

Predictive Decision Support: AI-powered systems that provide insights and recommendations to support decision-making, often based on predictive analytics.

Cognitive Computing: A branch of AI that aims to simulate human thought processes and enhance human decision-making.

Predictive Analytics: The use of data, statistical algorithms, and machine learning techniques to identify the likelihood of future outcomes based on historical data.

<u>Resource Allocation</u>: The process of distributing an organization's resources, such as budget, personnel, and equipment, to achieve strategic and operational goals.

<u>Inventory Management</u>: The practice of overseeing and controlling an organization's inventory to ensure efficient use of resources and meet customer demand.

<u>Route Optimization</u>: The use of algorithms and data analysis to identify the most efficient routes for transportation, reducing costs and improving delivery times.

<u>Customer Service Automation</u>: The use of AI-powered chatbots and virtual assistants to automate customer service tasks, such as responding to inquiries and providing support.

<u>Market Analysis</u>: The examination of market trends, consumer behavior, and competitive landscapes to inform strategic and operational decisions.

<u>Competitive Intelligence</u>: The gathering and analysis of information about an organization's competitors and the competitive environment to inform strategic decisions.

<u>Logistics and Supply Chain Management</u>: The process of planning, implementing, and controlling the efficient flow and storage of goods and services, including route planning and inventory management.

<u>Operational Efficiency</u>: The ability to carry out operational tasks with minimal waste and optimal use of resources.

<u>Agility</u>: The capacity to respond quickly and effectively to changing circumstances and emerging opportunities.

Risk Mitigation: Strategies and actions aimed at minimizing or managing potential risks to an organization.

Data-Driven Decisions: Making choices based on data analysis and insights rather than intuition or tradition.

Sustainability: The practice of conducting operations and making decisions that are environmentally and socially responsible.

Predictive Maintenance: The use of data and AI to predict when equipment or machinery is likely to fail so that maintenance can be performed just in time to prevent problems.

Blockchain: A distributed ledger technology that ensures transparency and security in data transactions.

Quality Control: Processes and measures implemented to maintain the quality of products or services.

Precision Demand Forecasting: Using AI to predict future demand for products or services with a high degree of accuracy.

Natural Language Processing (NLP): The technology that enables machines to understand, interpret, and generate human language.

Unlearning: The process of intentionally letting go of outdated or ineffective knowledge, beliefs, or behaviors to make room for new learning and adaptation.

Relearning: The act of acquiring new knowledge, skills, or behaviors to replace or update existing ones, often as a result of unlearning.

<u>Upskilling</u>: The process of acquiring additional skills or knowledge to enhance one's capabilities, usually for career advancement or adapting to changing job requirements.

<u>Reskilling</u>: The act of acquiring new skills or knowledge to transition into a different role or industry, often in response to job displacement or changing career paths.

This glossary provides a comprehensive reference to key terms and concepts covered in the book, including those related to unlearning, relearning, upskilling, and reskilling, ensuring clarity and understanding for readers

Bonus

As part of our commitment to supporting your organization's successful transition into the digital era, we are pleased to offer an exclusive bonus — the 'Strategic AI Skills Assessment for Workplace Excellence.'

This bonus is not just a tool; it's a catalyst for transformation. We believe in equipping you with what you need to lead your team effectively into the future, embracing the power of AI and operational and digital transformation.

This assessment is your key to understanding the strengths and areas for development within your organization, and it serves as the foundation for informed, targeted training and improvement initiatives.

By providing this bonus, we are empowering your organization to navigate the digital era with confidence and drive excellence within your workplace.

Let's embark on this transformative journey together, and unlock the potential of your team in the age of AI.

Strategic AI Skills Assessment for Workplace Excellence

Welcome to the "Strategic AI Skills Assessment for Workplace Excellence." In today's rapidly evolving business landscape, where operational and digital transformations are not merely buzzwords but strategic imperatives, it's essential to ensure that you and your team possess the right knowledge and skills.

This assessment is designed to provide insights into your understanding of key concepts related to strategic artificial intelligence (AI), operational and digital transformation, leadership, and ethical considerations. By participating in this assessment, you embark on a journey to evaluate and enhance your expertise in areas crucial for driving workplace excellence in the digital era.

In the following sections, you will encounter a series of carefully crafted questions and scenarios that will allow you to self-assess your proficiency in various aspects of strategic AI. We encourage you to answer each question honestly and thoughtfully. Your responses will help identify areas where you excel and areas that may benefit from further development.

As you complete this assessment, keep in mind that it's not just an evaluation of your current knowledge and skills; it's also an opportunity to set a course for your continuous learning and growth. Whether you find yourself well-versed in these topics or are just beginning your journey, this assessment is a tool for self-improvement and professional development.

Once you've completed the assessment, you will receive a summary of your strengths and areas for improvement. This information will guide your path to tailored training, mentorship, and resources that can empower you to lead with confidence in the age of AI.

We invite you to embrace this opportunity to evaluate, enhance, and unlock your strategic AI potential. Let's embark on this enlightening journey together and take a step closer to achieving workplace excellence in the digital era.

Now, let's get started.

1. Define the Training Goals:

Clearly outline the objectives of the assessment. What specific skills or knowledge areas are you looking to evaluate?

2. Select the Training Domains:

Identify the key areas relevant to your organization. For instance, in the context of your book, these might include operational transformation, digital transformation, AI strategy, and leadership.

3. Develop Assessment Questions:

Create a series of questions or scenarios related to each training domain. Ensure these questions are specific to the skills and knowledge you want to assess. For example:

"How familiar are you with operational transformation principles?"

"Can you explain the key components of a digital transformation strategy?"

"Do you understand the role of AI in workplace excellence?"

"Rate your leadership skills in driving digital transformation."

4. Use a Rating Scale:

Implement a rating scale for each question. For example:

"Not at all familiar"

"Somewhat familiar"

"Moderately familiar"

"Very familiar"

"Extremely familiar"

5. Include Open-Ended Questions:

In addition to rating questions, include open-ended questions that allow respondents to provide more detailed insights. For example:

"Please describe your experience with operational transformation in your current role."

"What challenges have you faced in implementing digital transformation initiatives?"

6. Determine Scoring Criteria:

Define the scoring criteria to evaluate the responses. For example, you might assign higher scores to more knowledgeable responses.

7. Data Analysis:

> Collect and analyze the responses to identify common skills or knowledge gaps among the participants.

8. Report and Recommendations:

> Create a report summarizing the assessment findings. Include recommendations for tailored training programs or resources based on identified gaps.

9. Implementation of Training:

> Implement training programs or initiatives based on the assessment results. These programs should be highly targeted to address the identified gaps and enhance the skills and knowledge of employees.

10. Ongoing Assessment:

> Periodically repeat the assessment to track progress and identify new training needs.

This tailored training assessment will help executives and organizations focus on specific skills and knowledge areas that are directly related to their strategic goals and the content of your book. It ensures that training efforts are efficient and aligned with organizational objectives.

Assessment Questions - These questions can be used or customized for your use.

1. How familiar are you with operational transformation principles?

2. Please rate your knowledge of digital transformation strategies.

3. On a scale of 1 to 5, how confident are you in your understanding of AI's role in workplace excellence?

4. How comfortable are you in leading teams through digital transformation initiatives?

5. Rate your ability to identify operational inefficiencies in your department.

6. How familiar are you with key AI technologies used in business operations?

7. Please rate your knowledge of strategies to enhance employee engagement during digital transformation.

8. On a scale of 1 to 5, how proficient are you in leveraging data analytics for strategic decision-making?

9. How experienced are you in implementing change management strategies during digital transformation?

10. Please rate your understanding of how AI can be ethically integrated into business operations.

Open-Ended Questions - These questions can be used or customized for your use.

1. Describe your experience with operational transformation in your current role.

2. Can you provide an example of a successful digital transformation initiative you've been involved in?

3. What specific challenges have you faced in implementing digital transformation projects?

4. How do you envision AI impacting workplace excellence in our organization?

5. What leadership skills do you believe are crucial for driving digital transformation effectively?

6. In your view, what are the key obstacles to operational efficiency in our department?

7. Share an instance where you've used AI technologies to improve a business process.

8. How do you currently engage and motivate your team during times of change or transformation?

9. Describe a situation where you used data analytics to inform a significant decision.

10. What ethical considerations do you think are most important when integrating AI into our operations?

Data Analysis:

Example of data analysis for a multiple-choice question:

For Question 1 ("How familiar are you with operational transformation principles?"), you could calculate the average rating across all responses to determine the general level of familiarity. For instance, if the average response is "3.5," it indicates a moderate level of familiarity.

Options for Using Assessment Data:

1. Customized Training: Tailor training programs based on identified gaps in knowledge and skills.

2. Mentoring and Coaching: Assign mentors or coaches to employees who need more guidance in specific areas.

3. Resource Recommendations: Provide employees with recommended reading materials, courses, or online resources related to their identified gaps.

4. Group Workshops: Organize workshops or seminars focused on specific areas that need improvement.

5. Skill-Building Exercises: Create exercises and projects that help employees practice and apply what they've learned.

6. Follow-Up Assessments: Periodically reassess to track progress and adapt training efforts.

7. Feedback Loops: Encourage employees to provide feedback on training initiatives to continually improve programs.

8. Career Path Planning: Use assessment data to inform career development and succession planning.

9. Performance Appraisals: Integrate training achievements and improvements into performance evaluations.

10. Strategic Planning: Utilize assessment data to shape organizational strategies and goals based on employee capabilities and needs.

These options help transform assessment data into actionable strategies for enhancing employee skills and knowledge.